The Miracle Diet for
Fast Weight Loss

The Miracle Diet for Fast Weight Loss

by

SIDNEY PETRIE

in association with

ROBERT B. STONE

With Special Forewords by

Milton C. Kemp, M.D., A.A.G.P.

and

J. Martin Seidenfeld, Ph.D.

PARKER PUBLISHING COMPANY, INC. West Nyack, N.Y.

PRINTED IN THE UNITED STATES OF AMERICA

To Iris, my slender wife

Sidney Petrie

Foreword
by a Doctor of Medicine

Mr. Sidney Petrie, nationally known author of the famous diet book *Martinis and Whipped Cream,* in his new book *The Miracle Diet for Fast Weight Loss* makes use of all the many great advances that have been made during the past few decades in the knowledge of human dietary requirements. These advancements contribute to the role nutrition plays in the maintenance of good health, weight reduction, and the prophylaxis of disease.

Practicing physicians such as myself are aware of the practical significance of essential nutrient intake in maintaining an adequate nutritional state of the body. Many individuals starve the body while gaining weight by depriving it of the essential nutrients and vitamins.

The distribution of meals is an extremely important factor in maintaining good health as well as aiding in weight reduction. Case histories obtained from numerous obese patients indicate that consumption of one huge meal per day is a very common occurrence.

The Miracle Diet for Fast Weight Loss, using these principles as well as many others, not only provides a safe, medically approved method of weight reduction but also a way of preventing the recurrence of excess poundage.

MILTON C. KEMP, *M.D., A.A.G.P.*
Medical Director of the New York Institute
for Hypnotherapy

3

Foreword
by a Clinical Psychologist

Most "diets" for losing weight fail. While the nutritional elements of a diet are usually carefully worked out so that the dieter's physical health needs are well provided for, the dieter's psychological needs are seldom even taken into account, except in a perfunctory way. Often, the dieter is reminded of the good that he (or more frequently, she) will be doing himself (herself). She is told that she will increase her longevity and will become more attractive to members of the opposite sex. But little thought is given to the psychological reality of the continuous sense of frustration that the dieter must experience.

Thus it was with great pleasure and surprise I read this latest book on losing weight by S. Petrie. For in it, he seems to have overcome the basic reasons that most dieters fail in their attempts to lose excess weight. Specifically, he demonstrates how easily anyone can alter his eating patterns, so that he can lose weight, maintain a satisfactory nutritional balance, and still satisfy his psychological needs. And it is these psychological needs that underlie the overeating patterns which led to these persons being overweight in the first place.

Like most original, but highly sensible programs, the solution presented here seems so obvious. Why has it not been implemented before? The answer, no doubt, is that few had really been aware of the problem, i.e., the psychological roots of obesity. And those that were aware—psychologists, psychiatrists, and other mental health professionals—knew little, and cared less, about sound nutrition and dieting.

In my opinion, this book represents a masterful synthesis, on a practical, workable level, of both the physical and the psychological factors of dieting for losing weight most effectively.

J. MARTIN SEIDENFELD, PH.D.

The Miracle That Awaits You

I Promise You
That Your Use of This Book Will . . .

- End the need for you to ever need to go on a diet again.
- Drop eight to fifteen pounds a month from your weight without ever feeling hungry.
- Add vigor and energy to your life.
- Restore your youthful, glowing look.
- End ailments related to overweight and dangerous diet pills you may be taking.
- Make physical body improvements for you at a speed that will astound you.
- Begin a new way of eating that will revitalize your body as you enjoy as many as six meals a day.
- Provide you with foods brimming with nutrients and natural vitamins.
- Improve your business, social and family life as you become a vital, aware person.
- Start an explosion of accomplishment as sluggish attitudes fade away.
- Make you sexually attractive.
- Make you a more effective person.
- Win friends you never had before.
- Replace sags, bulges and wrinkles with supple radiancy.
- Enable you to lose 10, 20, 50, even 100 pounds to restore your normal weight.
- Add healthful years to your life expectancy.

S. P.
R. B. S.

Contents

MIRACLE STEP FOUR   115

5. HOW TO COOK WHAT YOU LIKE, THE WAY YOU LIKE IT—AND LOSE WEIGHT . . . 116

The Calorie Limits • A Trustworthy Nutritional Barometer • The Miracle Protein Diet • All the Vegetables You Can Eat • The Mystery of Fresh Foods • Your Favorite Recipe May Have a Place on the Miracle Diet • Here Are Nearly 100 Exciting Recipes

MIRACLE STEP FIVE   155

6. HOW TO SELECT MIRACLE FOODS . . . 156

Foods That Pack a Nutritional Wallop for Weight Control • Why Proteins? • You Can Be Overweight and Under Nourished • How About That Evening Martini? • The Truth About Food Preservatives and Food Coloring • Foods with Life in Them • Grains That Nourish the Whole Body • Live Longer with Miracle Diet Foods • How to Prevent Iron Deficiency While Dieting • The World Is Your Supermarket

MIRACLE STEP SIX   171

7. HOW TO USE THE MIRACLE DIET TO RESTORE YOUTH 172

Can You Accept the Idea of Being Younger? • How to Think Thin and Young • One Minute a Day Can Take Years Off Your Appearance • How to

Reinforce the Mind's Role in Figure Control • Diet
Can Prolong Human Life • How to Enjoy a Radi-
ant, Youthful Skin • Coffee and Tea—Are They
Beneficial Beverages? • The Value of Food Supple-
ments • Food Supplements • You Can Postpone
Old Age for Decades

How Six Meals a Day Increases Sexual Potency •
Protein Affects Sexual Desire • The Tiny Gland
That Says Yes or No to Sex • The Gland That Acts
as Sexual Brake or Accelerator • Seeds and Sex •
How Vitamins Affect Sexual Activity • Minerals and
Sex Power • A Word of Advice to the Love-Lorn

The Model's Miracle Diet • Here Is the Model's
Miracle Diet A • The Health Spa Miracle Diet •
The Spa's Miracle Diet • The Career Girl's Sand-
wich Diet • The Miracle Sandwich Diet • The
Miracle Rice Diet • The Miracle Liquid Diet • For
Vegetarians Only • Here Is My Miracle Vegetable
Diet • Here Is the Miracle Fruit Diet • Other
Special Diets • The Person with Gourmet Tastes •
Children as Special People

MIRACLE STEP NINE   223

Some Problems That Face Miracle Dieters • The
Miracle Diet in a Nutshell • Skip Breakfast and
You Raid the Kitchen at Night • Snack If You Wish
and Lose Weight • Excerpts from the Miracle Diet
Mailbag • Thinking Habits Can Be as Fattening as
Eating Habits • Six Meals Are as Easy as Three •
The Most Important Ingredient in the Miracle Diet

The Miracle Diet for Fast Weight Loss

1

How This Diet Works Pounds-Off Miracles

We have all known that excessive weight is a villain. But few of us have ever known what to do about it.

Most diets are merely temporary measures. You soon gain back all you lost, and then some.

Except for one. And that is why I call it the Miracle Diet— with no argument from the hundreds of slender women that I have helped with it.

The secret of the Miracle Diet is that, unlike other diets, you don't starve and your body cells don't starve. You are just as well-fed at the end of the diet as you were when you started. So there is less motivation to bounce back by stuffing a "deprived" system with food.

Don't get me wrong. This is a no-nonsense diet—recommended by physicians[1]—that melts pounds off if you stick to it. It requires a willingness to make changes in your present eating habits. It takes discipline to carry out these changes.

---

[1] P. Fabry *et al.*, "Meal Frequency and Ischaemic Heart Disease," *The Lancet* (London: July 27, 1968) p. 190.

In return for these changes, I make you a significant promise: I promise you

- Six meals a day (not a type error—six meals every day while you lose)
- A variety of foods you can learn to like
- More vital minerals and vitamins than you may be eating now
- As many as five pounds a week off your weight
- A longer and happier life.

Is it a deal?
Then let's begin.

The Miracle Diet Has What Most Diets Lack

Remember when fish had a reputation for being "brain food"? That has never been substantiated, but recent experiments at Baylor University have found that mice can learn what other mice have been trained to do by being injected with an extract of their brain.

We may never find that kind of brain food for human beings, but there is no doubt that some foods supply very little nourishment to our vital organs while other foods are rich in essential nutrients that not only fortify the brain, but our heart, lungs, nerve tissue, muscles, blood and bones as well.

Harvard University's Nutrition Department is studying the feasibility of fortifying wheat in southern Tunisia and rice in rural Thailand with essential amino acids. These grains are the "staff of life" in those countries and, it is believed, such fortification will result in a marked increase in the protein quality of that diet.

Certain foods are protein, vitamin, and mineral-high. You can eat half the calories of these foods and come out twice as healthy.

I have built the Miracle Diet around these foods. You can eat much less of these foods and not feel hungry or deprived.

Mrs. L. M. wrote me a letter about a year after losing 60 pounds. She stated: "The Six Meal-a-Day Diet is my salvation.

I have my self-confidence back and my blood pressure has returned to normal. I am now leading a more productive life.
I do not have to constantly fight to stop myself from eating
and I no longer suffer from moods of depression."

Concentrated nutrition—six times a day—sounds like a weight
gain regime. The truth is, it melts the pounds off as calories are
confined to valuable foods and omitted on the foods of lesser value.

But how does it taste? Can I eat it and like it? Those questions
are answered by the simple expedient of providing a number of
diets that emphasize different foods for different tastes.

On the pages ahead are diets that glean the best from the foods
you know and like today; there are special diets for those who
lean toward fruits in their taste, or to vegetables, or to the meats,
cheeses, fishes. There is a liquid diet, a rice diet, even a sandwich
diet.

All are chock-full of teaming nutrients that make both men and
women "come alive" as they diet. They do just the opposite of
what most other diets do to starve the stomach and deplete the
body.

For example, take diets that recommend artificial sweeteners.

In one year, Americans consumed nearly 20 million pounds of
cyclamates, mostly in the form of low-calorie soft drinks. Now, of
course, cyclamates, by government order have been banned. In
Great Britain, several major food chains refuse to sell food or
beverages which have been treated with cyclamate, or saccharin or
dulein. Their reason: Research has shown these non-nutritive
sweeteners to be unsafe for animals.

The National Academy of Sciences advised that cyclamates
could be used in limited amounts. A regulation was then promptly
issued requiring labels to declare the content of cyclamate in the
product and limiting cyclamates from containing more than 25
parts per million of cyclohexylamine, the basic chemical in their
manufacture. Here is the inside story. Cyclamate breaks down
chromosomes in animals and these broken chromosomes have
been found in previous studies to be linked with tumors, bizarre
defects in newborn babies, and shortened life. These findings have
now been published by the Medical World News. In the fall of

1969 the U.S. Food and Drug Administration acted to ban cyclamates from general use.

Can you imagine the harm done to those human bodies who were not only short-changed on nutrients while dieting, but who had to combat large quantities of this unsafe chemical at the same time?

Another trial by diet suffered by millions of dieters is the slowdown of nutrients and the speed-up of diet pills.

Appetite depressants, dehydrators, and metabolic boosters tamper with the vital organs. They pick you up and let you down in a roller coaster fashion that yanks at the heart and innards at a time when their fuel has been cut down and their repair materials denied.

People get "hooked" on these pills and wonder why years later they are still taking them; why they need to take more and more of them as immunity builds up, and why they feel worse and worse instead of better and better.

Good nutrition can pull these people off the pill habit by giving their protein-starved body a new lease on life.

Conventional Diets as Aging Accelerators

Even without chemical sweeteners and diet pills, the conventional diets can sap your vitality by turning down, if not off, the flow of essential foods to the body's billions of cells.

There is evidence that once this is done to the body it is less able to utilize these essentials in the future. In other words, man can develop an immunity to his own proteins just as he does at old age. Repeated on-again, off-again dieting is that kind of a strain on the system. In other words, it can accelerate the aging process.

The Miracle Weight Loss Is Permanent Weight Loss

It seems almost ludicrous that the very reason we diet—to add to our longevity—can be the reason for shortening it. Yet that is the unhappy truth about melba toast and tea. Or many of the common diet foods. While the others are accomplices in the crime by reason of being part of diets that deplete the body and invite repeated diet cycles.

These repeated diet cycles and the damage they do can be avoided by one simple change in the approach:

Conventional diets are intended to *starve* the body.

The *Miracle Diet* is intended to *feed* the body.

That is a big difference. If you intend to starve the body, there must be a time limit on the event. The diet ends; the body begins its recovery from the ordeal.

On the other hand, if you intend to feed the body with a diet, there need be no time limit. You are doing what must be done normally. No sudden end of diet. No return to bad habits. Instead, an extension of the diet permanently without hardship, and with full satisfaction as a reconditioned way of eating.

Of course, this feeding must be controlled. If uncontrolled, you have the status quo—a scale groaning out the sad news of unwanted pounds.

The Secret Behind Six Meals a Day

I promised you six meals a day. This may sound like *over-*feeding the body, but it is really part of a workable control.

The purpose of this control is to feed the body precisely according to its needs. If the body receives less than it needs, it becomes depleted—and you look it. If the body receives more than it needs, it becomes over supplied—and you both look it and weigh it.

The ideal method of feeding a body is to supply it with the exact amount of food it needs, when it needs it.

Most herbivorous mammals, birds and other animals eat this way. It appears that they eat almost constantly. They have, in effect, 12 small meals a day instead of our three square meals a day.

What happens to animals when they are forced to eat like humans? It is reported by the *Nutritional Review,* in 1962, that every variety of animal becomes obese if forced to eat only two meals daily even though given an ideal diet.

The reason is simple. Most of the food is converted into energy for immediate use when small meals are eaten. If a woman expends

200 calories an hour during her waking hours, a 200-calorie meal every hour will be just right for immediate use.

None of the energy has to be stored as fat when it is supplied at the same rate that it is consumed.

Six 300-calorie meals can cause some people to lose weight, while three 600-calorie meals can cause them to gain. The total—1800 calories—is the same in either case, but the process of turning energy into fat has less of a chance to get started with six meals.

How Three Meals a Day Builds Fat

Most of the food you eat is converted into energy when small meals are eaten. You cannot see energy. It does not change dress sizes from 12 to 14 or men's collars from 15 to 15½. Energy just makes you feel energetic. You are able to do more and not feel tired.

On the other hand, when large meals are eaten, the body's enzyme systems are overwhelmed. There is just too much potential energy to be produced compared to what the body can use and too much compared to the body's capacity to convert it.

So a large portion of these big meals is stored as fat. And that is what happened to those animals in the experiment. Once they were put back on small frequent meals, their weight returned to normal.

Three meals a day build fat. But most Americans concentrate their daily food intake even more. They eat 80 percent of their food after 6 P.M.

A study of the eating habits of people who were having difficulty with their weight showed that they ate little throughout the day but did right well at dinner and during the evening.[2]

This calls out the body's full convert-to-fat team. In fact, that team has to work overtime as the consumption of energy declines at bedtime.

We are really eating the most when we need it the least. A big breakfast and hardly any dinner would be more in tune with the demand.

If you were your body what would you do with a bowl of pea

---

[2] A. J. Stunkard *et al., American Journal of Medicine*, Vol. 63 (July 15, 1955).

soup aux croutons, a half pound of pot roast with gravy, some mashed potatoes, salad, apple pie and coffee? You have plenty of time to decide. The demand for fuel is down to a minimum for eight hours.

No, six meals a day is not feeding the body too much, too often. It is avoiding the overtaxing of the body by spreading out the fuel supply to conform more closely to the body's demand for it. It is feeding the body what it needs when it needs it.

How a Missed Meal Can Build Fat

The body likes to get fuel as it needs it. If it doesn't, the blood sugar falls, causing symptoms with which most overweight people are only too familiar: fatigue, hunger, irritability, headache.

With these symptoms comes a craving for sweets. If this is not satisfied, then the person is likely to overeat at the next meal. Candy binge or triple portions—take your pick. No matter what the choice, it adds up to unwanted fat.

But that's not the end of the story.

When excessive sweets or other carbohydrates are consumed, they are absorbed so rapidly that a healthy pancreas is overstimulated. It produces not only enough insulin to convert the excess sugar into fat, but it keeps on producing insulin and even converts the normal supply of blood sugar into fat also, thus causing a shortage of blood sugar.

Another shortage of blood sugar means another hungry person. And the cycle of overeating continues.

A missed meal causes excess fat because of a pendulum action. The blood sugar level in this case is the pendulum. And when it swings it creates hunger at one end and fat on the other.

The Miracle Diet keeps the blood sugar pendulum from swinging. It keeps the blood sugar at a closer to constant level.

It is really no miracle. Just natural, common sense.

How Devitalized Foods Can Build Fat

Recently a woman came to me who claimed she was on an 800 calorie diet and was not losing weight. Now, I have seen cases such as this time and time again, and I knew there was one of two possible answers:

- Either she was fooling herself and really eating more
- Or she was eating mostly sweets and starches.

I gave her a chart to help her keep an accurate diary of everything she ate or drank for one week. When I saw her the following week we added up the calories each day. She was close to right. The average was 875. I put her on the scales. Her weight had not budged—148 lbs.

Then I checked the menu.

The reason was certainly obvious! She starved herself all day for a spaghetti dinner. She ate a salad for one evening meal plus two servings of chocolate layer cake. One day she lived on jelly sandwiches. I figured that her 875 daily calories consisted of 90 percent pure sugar and starch.

These carbohydrates are known as quick energy foods. But what is not known as universally is that the body needs certain nutrients to run this energy-creating process. If it does not get these nutrients, then the energy cannot be created no matter how much quick energy sugar is consumed.

So the body slows down. The metabolic rate of the body processes drops. Less energy is expended. More is converted to fat.

I upped this woman's daily intake to 1150 calories—and she began to lose weight. These were nutritional calories—rich in protein, vitamins and minerals.

Fat is lost only when energy is being produced by the body. It follows that weight cannot be lost unless fat is effectively burned, a process requiring many vital nutrients.

A lack of any of the B vitamins causes a marked lag in energy production. Y. J. Kotake discovered in 1955 that rats without vitamin B_6 utilized both protein and fat so ineffectively they became grossly obese. Throttle the supply of pantothenic acid and fat burns at only half the normal rate. Vitamin E added to a diet formerly deficient in it or in protein causes the rate of utilization of fat to double.[3] Protein itself is needed for a host of energy-producing enzymes.

---

[3] C. Artom, *American Journal of Clinical Nutrition,* Vol. 6, No. 221 (1958); and H. D. Alexander, *Journal of Nutrition,* Vol. 61, No. 329 (1957).

The Importance of Protein in Weight Loss

I consider protein the most important of all nutrients in the burning of fat. I don't mean to the exclusion of others, but if I had to prepare a list of priorities I would place protein at the top.

Protein foods, as you know, include meats, fish, cheese, eggs, and poultry. I have discussed their dramatic effects in body weight loss in previous books (*Martinis and Whipped Cream* and also *How to Reduce and Control Your Weight Through Self-Hypnotism*).

Proteins act just the opposite of carbohydrates. They give you slow constant energy instead of a sudden surge that peters out. Also, they step up the metabolic rate of the body, instead of slowing it down. With metabolism at a higher clip, more energy is utilized and more fat is burned off.

Proteins are the body's building blocks. The body needs these building blocks just to keep in repair. As cells die, and millions die in the body every day, they must be replaced with new cells. This takes protein and lots of it.

In areas of the world where proteins are scarce, no amount of other foods will prevent the inevitable deterioration of the body that occurs. The reason protein is on the top of my list of nutrients is that that's where nature puts it, too.

Perhaps by design, nature has made proteins the most appetizing and tasteful foods. You will find them in many savory and tempting dishes in the diets presented on the pages ahead.

How Oil May Chase Fat Out of the Body

One of the first things that the average diet cuts out or down is oil and fat. Over a decade ago, however, a test was made on hospital patients given different diets, all with the same number of calories, but only one of the diets contained any oil.[4]

The patients on the diet with some oil were able to stay with their diet most easily. They not only lost weight but did not regain their lost weight as long as the oil was continued.

---

[4] J. H. Fryer *et al.*, *Journal of Laboratory and Clinical Medicine*, Vol. 45, No. 684 (1955).

Oils have a way of decreasing hunger, too. They appear to retard the emptying time of the stomach. They also stimulate the burning of body fat and this keeps blood sugar at normal levels for longer periods.

"Standard" reducing diets cut out all oil and fat wherever possible. This, I believe, is a contributing factor to their general failure to reduce weight successfully.

I insist on a little oil every day. Salad dressing for instance, with oil, is a contributing factor to the success of the Miracle Diet. How much oil and when?—Read on.

Miraculous Health Dividends of Six Meals a Day

Recently Dr. P. Fabry, head of the physiology department of the Institute of Human Nutrition at Prague, Czechoslovakia, reported that he found that men who ate three square meals a day tended toward overweight as compared with patients who ate five or more smaller meals.

He discovered something else: men who ate three square meals had impaired blood sugar levels and high cholesterol levels by the time they reached 60 to 64 years of age. In fact, while over 30 percent of the three-meal-a-dayers in the 1100 men he studied in this age bracket had ischemic heart disease, less than 20 percent of the subjects eating five or more meals a day suffered from the heart ailment.

Now, Dr. Fabry did not pretend to know why. In fact, he emphasized that the experiment could not possibly prove whether the low number of meals caused heart disease or whether the larger number of daily meals prevented it.

The fact is important though that *five or more meals a day proved to be a healthier way of life.*

I have seen it improve health and restore youthful vigor in both men and women, and of all ages.

"I feel lighter on my feet as if free of a load I was carrying," was the way a 32-year-old housewife put it.

"Big dinners seem to have given me a middle-age paunch. Now it's gone," said a 41-year-old bank executive after five weeks of six meals a day.

Illustration A—BEFORE

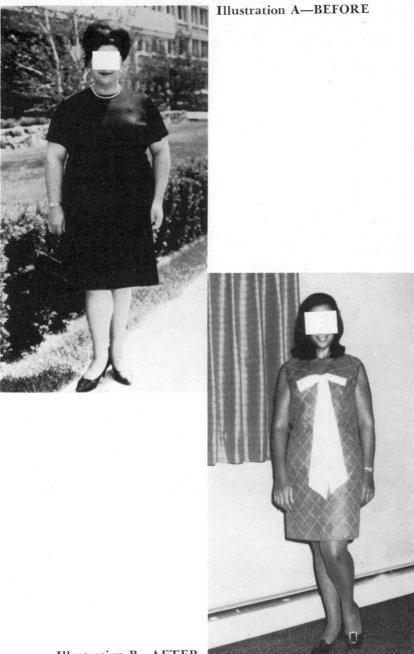

Illustration B—AFTER

"I've never felt better. I've been on and off diets for 20 years, always thinking that the fewer meals the better. This is a miracle." A 38-year-old teacher spoke these words standing on a scale that read 12 pounds lost in three weeks.

For many of the men and women who have been referred to me by physicians, the Miracle Diet has been an astonishing experience. Let me show you in "before and after" pictures how one of my clients lost 108 pounds with the Miracle Diet. See Illustrations A and B.

It seems to go contrary to what we have been taught and come to believe. Logic seems to dictate that to lose weight one must eat fewer meals. Logic seems to dictate also that the food in those fewer meals should be scanter, not richer, in nutrients. And who would think that a little fat is better than none at all?

Yet it works.

A DIABETIC FINDS A DIET SHE CAN STAY ON

Mrs. G., a diabetic, was notorious for not being able to stay on a diet. She always claimed constant hunger in the evening.

Her physician and I worked out a six-meal Miracle Diet especially tailored to her. It ran about 1,000 calories.

After the first week, she weighed in at five pounds less. I waited for the expected barrage of complaint. It didn't come. "How do you feel about this diet?" I asked, not being able to stand the suspense. She replied, "I am satisfied plus."

Mrs. G. said that the six meals gave her the "inner strength" not to overstep the bounds one little bit.

Later she wrote me, "I am recommending your diet to other diabetics. I cannot understand why many people do not take advantage of this diet for their appearance and for their health."

Many who promised themselves they would never try another reducing plan again saw the results, tried it themselves, and are now rejoicing in their new-found slender look.

While they eat twice as many meals as they did before, fatty bulges disappear as pounds vanish from legs, hips, thighs, stomach, arms, neck and face. For many it has been not only a miracle, but a dream come true.

There are many psychological advantages to eating twice as often. Eating has a psychological function for everybody and especially for those who are overweight. The wife who nags her husband about the "tire" around his middle is only driving him to food. Women who are "down" because of their unattractive figure tend to "lose" themselves in more frequent trips to the refrigerator.

Six meals a day nourishes the psyche, as well as the body. It avoids putting the dieter out on a psychological limb as is so often the case with standard "starvation" regimes.

You eat often and you enjoy a feeling of well-being.

The Diet Racket

It is estimated that there are 50 million overweight Americans and that they spend over $250 million a year on weight reduction schemes.

The drug industry, the medical profession, even bakeries are "living off the fat of the land." Belts that hold in your abdomen, exercise wheels, and stomach "fillers" are the latest gimmicks on the market.

The amount of diet foods and diet drinks that are marketed annually stagger the imagination. The pounding by masseurs, the jogging, the vibrating of mechanical vibrators could literally shake the earth.

One of the latest products of the fat-fighting industry is the summer camp. There are now an estimated 300 camps in the country that cater specifically to overweight teenagers. Fees for eight weeks run between $500 and $1,000. Some guarantee 20 to 50 pound losses to campers. And they deliver. Sweating teenagers engage in physical activities every day. They are cut to 1200 calorie diets. Some have dropped 60 pounds in the two months.

There's a catch. Only 60 percent maintain their weight loss for at least a year. Many of the customers are "regulars," summer in and summer out, year in and year out.

Many physicians throw up their hands about the prospect of losing weight and staying thin. There is a defeatist school of thought that once fat always fat, that overweight is a condition that takes over at an early age and cannot be dislodged.

On the other hand, physicians who specialize in obesity have formed the American Society of Bariatrics. They believe that education and discipline can eventually transform an overweight person into a permanently slender person.

There is no doubt in my mind that anybody can lose weight and stay slim. I see it happen year in and year out in my practice. But it cannot be done by discipline alone, and education in discipline has until now led to many a "dead end" in the search for permanent weight loss.

The *diet*—as it is commonly known—is an error. It is perhaps one of the biggest, most prolonged errors made by mankind. The ups and downs that diets have caused in recent generations, compounded by the overweight born of their failures, may have caused more fatalities and cut more years off life expectancy than possibly any other cause.

The Basic Error of Conventional Reducing Diets

The error of "diet" lies in its basic precept—temporary deprivation of nourishment. It is a false precept. One cannot get thin by temporary deprivation, no matter how long or short the time.

You cannot get thin by depriving your body of breakfast or any other meal. You make it up the next time.

You cannot get thin by depriving your body over a period of weeks or months. You make it up as soon as the period ends.

You can get thin by providing the body with exactly what nutrients it needs. No more. No less.

I admit that there is much the world has to learn about nutrition. Despite the great attention given to this subject, it is so vast that the ground has been barely covered. A simple process like the digestion of protein is not fully understood. Nor do we understand why some people react one way to certain foods and other people quite a different way to the same foods.

It is high time that many of the professions and industries ministering to the overweight populace devote some portion of their annual "take" to nutrition research. Perhaps these additional funds and the findings they produce can reinforce our education of the overweight with valid ways for lifetime control.

This research is already uncovering the startling fact that eating more frequently, not less frequently, is the proper way to eat.

My clinical applications of these findings prove them to be correct. Through this book, I share with you the joyous experiences of those slenderized six-meal-a-day men and women.

The Promise of This Book

Alice M., 26, is an average young housewife. She has had two children and each time has emerged heavier. When I first saw her, she weighed 154 and called herself "slightly overweight." She admitted that when she married five years before, she was a slim 122.

I could cite actresses, society's "400," models who have thinned with me, but I mention Alice because I was her first resort, not her last. She had never seriously dieted before and she was anxious now to be successful on the first try.

It took 11 weeks, less than three months, and she was back to 122. Was it a nightmare? Did she starve? Had she earned the bronze star for bravery? "What's all the fuss about dieting," she asked when she left. "It was a breeze."

It is now two years later and Alice is still in the low 120's. When I phoned her, as I often do to get follow-up records years later, she said she had just finished her second lunch.

Yes, Alice is still eating six meals a day.

And there are hundreds of Alices—women who have had permanent success with the Miracle Diet. Their success is its promise to you.

On the pages ahead, you will find a step by step guide to the Miracle Diet. It tells you:

> how to begin
> how to plan six meals a day
> how to eat six meals at work or at home
> how to recognize the right foods
> how to cook for best nutrition
> how to limit calories painlessly

how to enjoy food to the fullest
how to control your weight loss
how to stay thin.

I have supplied you with all you need to know in this book—a score of diets for every taste, six-meal menus for multiple weeks, calorie counts on hundreds of popular foods, and dozens of gourmet recipes for high nutritional dining. But only one miracle:

The permanently slender YOU.

Miracle Step One

Look at yourself in a full length mirror. Face forward. Then turn and look at your full length profile. With the additional help of a hand mirror, get a full length rear view.

Stay there and look one, two, three minutes or longer, until you build up a compelling conviction that "it's time for a change."

Resolve that you will treat this only body you have with love and concern—that you will eat less for mental satisfaction and more for bodily need.

2

How to Begin
the Miracle Diet

When I tell a man or woman who has come to me to help them lose weight that the hardest thing they are going to have to learn to do is double up on their meals, you can imagine the look I get.

Yet, it's true.

We are all creatures of habit and if we are accustomed to three square meals a day, it is going to be an uphill fight to stick conscientiously to a six-meal regime.

A skipped meal in this diet is likely to mean weight gain, not weight loss. Because when you miss a meal, you are going to be hungrier when the next meal arrives and you will eat more—more than the body needs and it may be stored as fat.

We want to put the body's fat-making *machinery* into storage, not the fat. We want to feed our body at the rate our body needs food, slower, if anything, not faster—so the fat-making can stop, and the fat breaking begin.

The Ex-Model Who Dropped 48 Pounds and the "Ex"

When I tried to explain this to a 22-year-old former television commercial model who had grown to such proportions that the only products left for her to plug might be diet concoctions and exercise gadgets, she laughed.

"That's how I got this way," she said, "eating six meals a day."

Of course, she was talking about six different meals. To help make this point I asked her to describe a typical day. It went something like this:

9:30 A.M. Orange juice, coffee
12:30 P.M. Club sandwich, pie, coffee
3:00 P.M. Coffee and cake
6:00 P.M. Cocktails with canapes or snacks
8:00 P.M. Soup, entree, salad, dessert, coffee
11:30 P.M. Sandwich, beer.

If you were sitting in the office with me at the time, and had previously read this far in this book, how would you criticize this ex-model's eating pattern? Look at it from the point of view of timing, quantity, type, etc.

Let's look at the timing. She was a late riser and did not bother with breakfast until she was ready to leave the apartment. Then she downed some juice and poured herself a cup of black coffee. She called that meal No. 1.

I call it mistake No. 1. Why, in a minute.

Her timing was about three hours apart. Now this was fine. Except . . .

Her meals got bigger as the day went on and she wound up with a meal just before retiring. Little did she realize as she sat there in front of me that most of her 48 surplus pounds were produced while she was asleep.

What about type of food? You can see because she was a gal on the go she favored sandwiches, cakes, pies. These are heavy in carbohydrates, light in the proteins that nourish the body, and light in the vitamins and minerals that revitalize the body—morning juice and dinner salad excepted.

Mistake No. 1 was in not providing a more substantial start to the day so as to maintain blood sugar levels and head off hunger.

Mistake No. 2 was in not providing more nutritious foods and fewer sweets and starches that turn so readily into fat.

Mistake No. 3 was in providing too much food at the end of the day and before retiring.

Had Miss Ex-Model not made these three mistakes she would probably still be modeling. But now that she had amassed 48 pounds as a result of these mistakes, she would not only have to correct them but discipline herself quantity-wise to lose unwanted poundage.

She chose to go on the "Weight Smasher" six-meal diet—the one requiring the most discipline of the four that I provide you with later.

In three weeks the scale read down from 160 to 147.

In three more weeks she had blasted off another 12 pounds. It took a total of 13 weeks, a typical TV contract period, to get back to a semblance of a model. She went from a 39 inch bust to 35, from a 28 inch waist to 24 and from 38 inch hips to 35½.

And she went from an ex-model to a model for several nationally sold home products.

When to Eat Six Meals During a Day

You may not have as easy a time of it as our model friend. She had already developed the habit of eating six meals a day. All she had to do was shift the times—and the size. Most people eat three times a day. If they eat in between these meals, they don't call that type of eating a meal. It's a snack or a coffee break or a tea or cocktails or a nightcap.

The first step in starting the Miracle Diet is to recognize that every time you eat, you are eating a meal. There are no snacks or coffee breaks—just six meals a day. There are no teas or cocktail hours—just six meals a day.

Each period of eating and drinking becomes as important as the one before and the one after.

To help accomplish this recognition of six meals a day, I always insist that we drop the names that we have given these off-meal repasts, and substitute new names in their place.

From now on you will be having a:

    FIRST BREAKFAST
    SECOND BREAKFAST
    FIRST LUNCH

Second Lunch
First Dinner
Second Dinner

The two breakfasts will have all the characteristics of your present breakfasts. The two lunches will be similar in nature to your present lunches. The two dinners will be more like your present dinner split into two sittings.

You may find breakfasts add up to more than you may be eating while you gained weight. You are quite likely to find that the two dinners add up to less than your present evening's fare.

The reason for this shift in emphasis is obvious when you look at the Miracle Diet in the light of its basic idea: a conveyor belt feeding coal into the furnace only as fast as the energy is needed to run the machine—and no faster.

How fast does the human machine utilize energy? Taking the calorie as a unit of energy, man is said to burn an average of 3000 calories a day. A calorie in the language of physics is the amount of energy which is needed to raise the temperature of one grain of water one degree Centigrade. In diatetics, the calorie value of food derives in a general way from this initial definition, but since no two people convert energy from food at the identical rate of efficiency, the value is not absolute as it is in physics.

Three thousand calories a day can vary widely for different people. Here are some rules of thumb:

Men burn more calories per day than women.
Larger persons burn more than smaller.
Physically active people burn more.
Mentally active people burn more than their opposites at the same level of physical activity.
People burn more while awake than while asleep.
People with high metabolism rates burn more.

Thus a 250-pound lumberjack may burn 3600 calories over a 24-hour period compared to 2400 calories for a 100-pound stenographer.

Since one pound of human flesh will produce 3500 calories of energy, a person's daily consumption of energy dictates his maximum weight loss.

The lumberjack would lose more than a pound a day if he did not eat at all. The stenographer on a strict fast would lose about two-thirds of a pound a day. Of course, both would have to continue to exert themselves in their work at the same rate as before.

Don't panic. No one is going on a fast or even a starvation diet. There are six wholesome meals a day ahead for everyone, no matter how fast you wish to lose.

However, the rate of calorie consumption is important as it enables us to time our six meals as well as plan their size.

Let's take our stenographer again. She utilizes 2400 calories a day. Now if these were divided evenly, awake or asleep (which they are not), she would need 200 calories an hour. This could mean six 400-calorie meals every four hours.

But since a person cannot eat a meal while asleep we have to do some juggling.

She has to eat her six 400-calorie meals during her 16 waking hours. This means a meal on arising and the other five at three-hour intervals.

For office workers, housewives, and other women whose day is fairly uniform in energy expenditure, this even spacing of the meals would satisfy our conveyor belt concept—and keep energy going in at the same rate that it is going out.

For men in similar constant and uniform situations, the same would be true: a meal on arising and the other five at approximate three-hour intervals.

Such a schedule might be that shown in the table below. I call it the *Basic Schedule*.

BASIC SCHEDULE

First Breakfast	—	7:00 a.m.
Second Breakfast	—	10:00 a.m.
First Lunch	—	1:00 p.m.
Second Lunch	—	4:00 p.m.
First Dinner	—	7:00 p.m.
Second Dinner	—	10:00 p.m.

This is a typical six-meal-a-day schedule, one which you might want to shoot for, but there are other factors to consider.

How to Ease the Pressure on Your Body to Store Fat

Six meals evens out the supply of energy to your body. Twelve meals could even out even better. A conveyor belt of spoonfuls traveling slowly while you were resting, speeding up three hours before you became active, and slowing down again three hours before you rested again—if totaling as many calories as you expended —would never present the body with the need to store excess calories as fat.

To help illustrate how this pressure for fat storage can be lessened, I have prepared several diagrams. These are purely symbolic and theoretical. They are not meant to be technical, medical, or physiological. I'm afraid there are too many charts and diagrams in the medical libraries, and I do not intend to add to what amounts to confusion for the average person. So I have tried to oversimplify what can be complicated concepts.

I have mentioned the conveyor belt keeping up with calorie utilization. Diagram 2-1 shows this calorie utilization for typical people—the active and inactive male, and the active and inactive female. This is one oversimplification, because no two people are exactly alike in their energy expenditure.

Here's another oversimplification.

Note that there are only two levels of calorie utilization shown —waking and sleeping. Actually this calorie utilization differs from hour to hour, even minute to minute. However, the minor ups and downs do not affect the problem or the outcome and what the straight line does is to indicate the average level, and help us to visualize the conveyor belt concept.

This idea of a conveyor belt is illustrated in Diagrams 2-2, 2-3, and 2-4. They show how food intake, if averaged over waking hours, would compare for an active female.

2-2. with a stable weight condition (2700 calories)
2-3. with a weight gain   (3700 calories)
2-4. with a weight loss   (1700 calories)

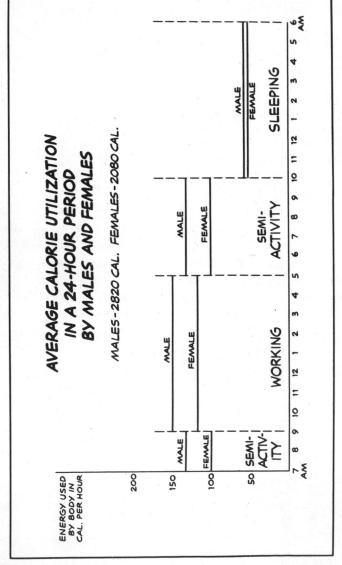

Diagram 2-1

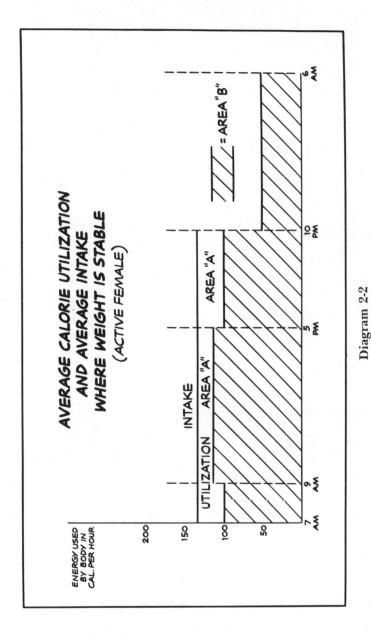

AVERAGE CALORIE UTILIZATION
AND AVERAGE INTAKE
WHERE WEIGHT IS STABLE
(ACTIVE FEMALE)

= AREA "B"

AREA "A"

AREA "A"

INTAKE

UTILIZATION

ENERGY USED
BY BODY IN
CAL. PER HOUR

200

150

100

50

7
AM

9
AM

5
PM

10
PM

6
AM

Diagram 2-2

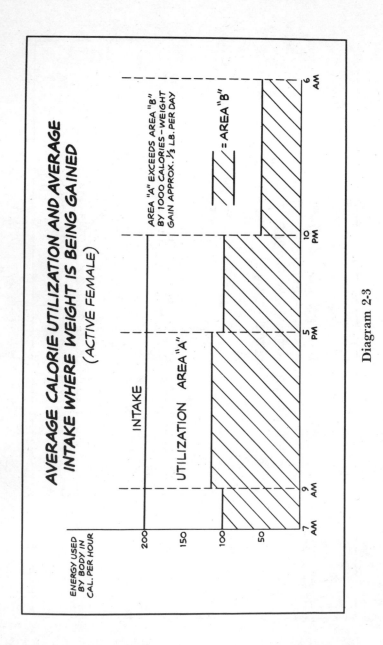

Diagram 2-3

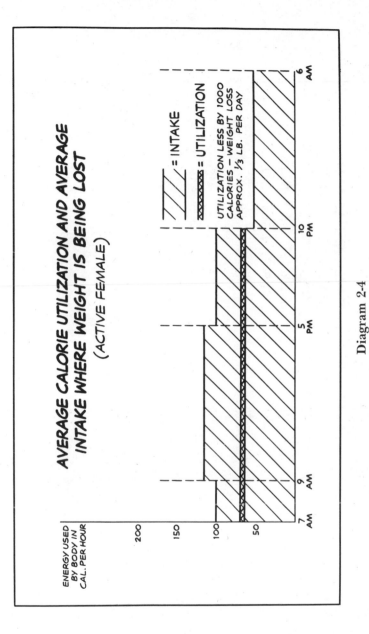

Diagram 2-4

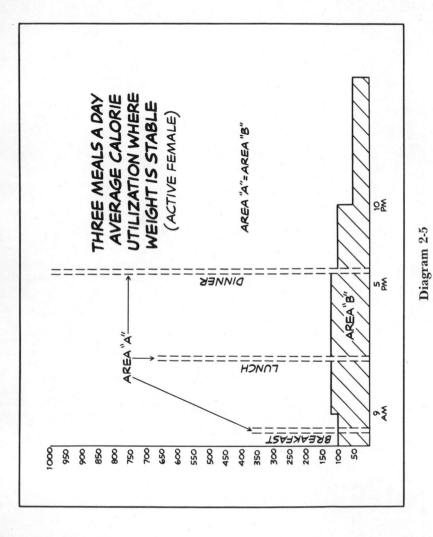

Diagram 2-5

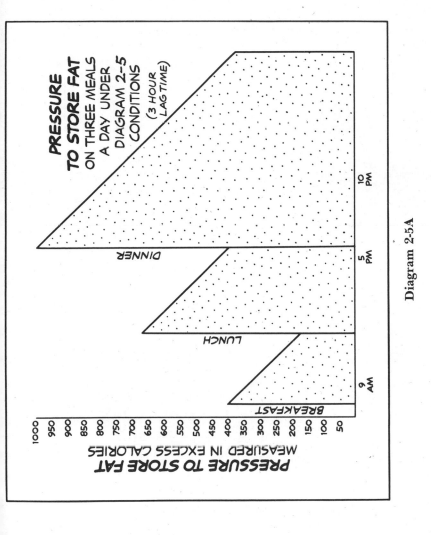

Diagram 2-5A

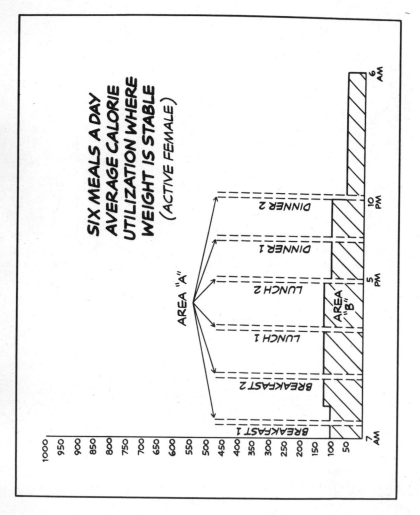

Diagram 2-6

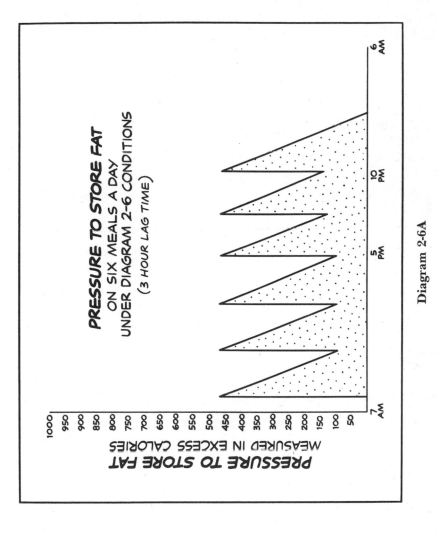

PRESSURE TO STORE FAT
ON SIX MEALS A DAY
UNDER DIAGRAM 2-6 CONDITIONS
(3 HOUR LAG TIME)

PRESSURE TO STORE FAT
MEASURED IN EXCESS CALORIES

Diagram 2-6A

In Diagram 2-2, you can see that the "intake" line, which could represent the conveyor belt, provides slightly more calories per hour than the utilization rate. This provides a margin for the body's period of sleep. Actually, the total calories of intake represented by the area under the dotted intake line (Area "A") is equal to the total calories utilized, represented by the area under the solid utilization line (Area "B").

The white rectangle between the two lines has special significance.

Can you tell what it is?

It would not exist if intake could be at the same rate as utilization, that is, if the conveyor belt could operate all night. But it must get ahead during the day in order to provide a supply at night. The white area is the calories stored.

Look what happens when too many calories are consumed (Diagram 2-3).

Now, with 1000 calories more to store than are utilized, the area between the two lines is much larger.

Suppose calorie intake was 1000 less than calories utilized. Will the area be less? You can bet it will, as shown in Diagram 2-4.

Here the need to store is reduced to almost no need at all. There are still slightly more calories supplied during the waking hours, and these are stored in the blood as a higher blood sugar level.

More Meals Equal Less Pressure to Store Fat

In some hospital rooms you can see a conveyor belt in action. This is when intravenous feeding is necessary and a liquid flow is controlled from a bottle so that it drips nourishment at a steady rate into the blood stream.

But the rest of us eat. We usually eat three times a day. So instead of one straight intake line, in reality our intake line is represented by three short high-level lines.

Diagram 2-5 shows this typical three-meal-a-day intake for our active female who is not gaining or losing. Each meal is 900 calories, equaling 2700 at the end of the day, her exact utilization. So there is no weight gain, no weight loss.

But there is still a pressure on the body to store calories as fat. This pressure is illustrated in Diagram 2-5A, where the excess calorie level is shown. Note how it rises after each meal. The area under this line (shaded) is the total pressure to store fat in calorie-hours.

Now let's see what happens to this pressure to store fat when we eat half as much, twice as often, as indicated in Diagrams 2-6 and 2-6A.

With peaks of intake reaching to less of a calorie height, we find the shaded area in Diagram 2-6A noticeably less than in Diagram 2-5A.

Six meals a day cuts the pressure on the body to store calories as fat.

What the Body Does When It Is Fed Excess Calories

In neither the three-meal or six-meal examples given above did our active female gain weight. This means that the body had a safety valve to relieve the pressure to store excess calories as fat.

The fact is, our bodies have more than one such safety valve. The one used most often is the blood sugar level. This rises to accommodate moderate, temporary oversupplies.

However, when the oversupply of calories is neither moderate nor temporary, this safety valve cannot handle the problem. Another safety valve is often brought in. It is the stepping-up of the metabolic rate. In effect, the furnace burns faster in an effort to consume the excess.

There are other safety valves, perspiration, elimination, etc., but science is not very familiar with how and when they operate, largely due to wide individual differences.

Eventually, the safety valves are no longer adequate to the increased pressure and the body yields to that pressure and creates fat.

This can happen in a year, a week, or overnight. For some people it happens with the slightest pressure of excess calories. Their safety valves just don't seem to be able to handle it.

For others, a weekend of wining and dining will barely budge the scale and, as long as it gives way to five days of calm, the threat

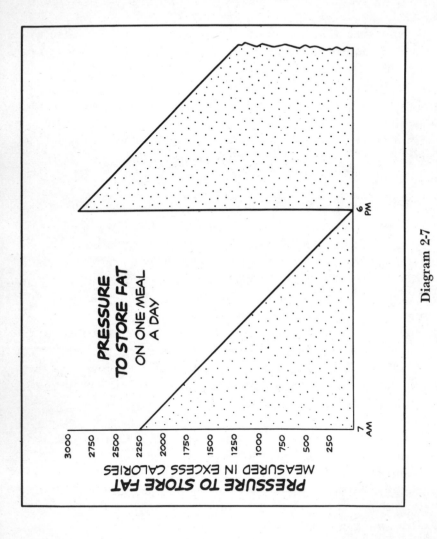

Diagram 2-7

is over. Their safety valves can handle thousands of excess calories for days without an ounce of fat stored.

And then of course there are those envied people who never seem to gain no matter what they eat. They go through life forever slim. Their safety valves seem so efficient that their body has thrown away the key to the fat making machinery. Their excess calories are used or eliminated—never stored.

Whatever your tolerance is for excess calories, you approach that limit *less* frequently when you eat *more* frequently.

Remember the greater shaded area under the three-meal-a-day excess calorie graph as compared to the six-meal-a-day graph? How do you think it would look with one meal a day? See Diagram 2-7.

One meal a day builds up an even greater pressure on the system to create fat storage. The blood sugar will rise, the body temperature may go up, the pulse rate may increase, perspiration may flow, and the bowels and kidneys may work overtime.

However, the fat making machinery may still have to begin to hum.

The Hottentots, who live in South Africa and depend largely on wild game for their survival, may go several days without a meal. Then when they make a kill they eat like it was going out of style. It may be their one meal in three days. What do you think their curve of excess calories looks like? And what do you think the body does about it?

The Hottentot's body gives into the pressure to build fat, and builds it. They have humps of fat around their buttocks that act pretty much like the camel's hump to store in times of plenty for use in the days ahead.

Would you like to go on such a diet? How about one large meal every six days? Goodbye waistline; goodbye wardrobe.

How to Limit Excess Calories
Without Cutting Down on Food

You can see that the effect on the body of big meals is practically the same as constant overeating, even though those big meals might be far apart.

You are loading the body with excess calories and asking the body to store them.

You are probably already thinking about your new regime of six meals a day to cut that need for storage. And you may also be thinking about some fine points in regulating those meals to cut the storage needs even further.

For instance, remembering the rising peaks of storage in Diagrams 2-5A and 2-6A, you might already be thinking that meals ought to diminish as the day wears on, not increase.

This is absolutely true.

Unfortunately, we eat small breakfasts in this era, and large dinners. The large dinners are especially detrimental as they add calories just when the demand is being stepped down.

Dr. William G. Shipman reported in the *Ladies Home Journal* recently that overweight people usually stay up late at night and eat after other members of the family have gone to bed.

Up goes the storage level, even higher.

Dr. Shipman, who is chief clinical psychologist at Chicago's Michael Riese Hospital, recommended that overweight wives go to bed at the same time as their husbands like normal weight women do.

What he is instructing, besides eating less, is that normal weight women eat their last meal several hours before retiring, rather than several minutes before retiring.

You can cut down on other temporary overages by tailoring the time between meals. But remember the three hour time lag in setting schedules:

It takes an average of three hours from the time a meal is consumed for it to be converted into available energy.

So, if your period of greatest activity is early afternoon, you would space meals closer together in the period beginning three hours before, making them two hours apart instead of three.

What to Do About an Irregular Day

Many people do not find that their working day is uniform. Some women like to do their housework and marketing in the morning and socialize in the afternoon. They use more energy in the morning, less in the afternoon.

Some jobs require more energy at one time of the day than another. A school bus driver can do a three-hour stretch in the early morning and another three-hour stretch in the early afternoon. For such people the Basic Schedule may have to be changed.

The conveyor belt can answer this greater energy demand in two ways:

It can carry more food
It can move the same food faster.

Translating this into our six meals a day, it means that at high energy periods of the day we can either:

Eat a larger meal
     or
Eat more frequently.

Larger Meals Are Out!

Larger meals take us in the wrong direction—the direction which leads to overweight, as indicated by the Prague study referred to in the first chapter.

Therefore, the six meals must be spaced closer together, not wider, when energy is needed.

Important fact: It takes three hours for food that enters the mouth to travel that conveyor belt into the furnace. So schedule adjustments must be made to prove a *lead time of three hours.*

You should tailor the Basic Schedule to your own personal energy requirements. Exactly how to do this is spelled out in a future chapter.

Meanwhile, you should start the Miracle Diet by going on a six-meal regime as close to the Basic Schedule as your family or business life permits.

Importance of Meal No. 1 and Meal No. 6

When you first arise in the morning, your blood sugar is at a comfortable energy level because it has usually not been drained at night as it would be during active daytime hours. That is why most people are not as hungry for breakfast as they are for dinner.

This is a trap for your weight reducing program.

People who are overweight are often those who have fallen into this very trap. They feel they can skip breakfast because they do not have the hunger pangs that caused them to eat so heartily the evening before.

Skipping breakfast causes a *drain on the blood sugar level* as activity and exertion takes place. Result: a cycle of hunger and overeating produces an oscillating or up and down blood sugar level that tends to perpetuate this cycle.

The Miracle Diet demands breakfast.

It not only requires a nutritional breakfast but it requires that it be enjoyed as soon as you rise.

Meal No. 1 should be eaten, if possible, even before dressing and other morning rituals. This will help insure that its energy will be available to your bloodstream before existing blood sugar levels are too depleted. Remember it takes three hours before this breakfast can turn into fuel for the conveyor belt. Remember, too, that this is one of those oversimplifications.

Meal No. 6 is important because it probably will determine how high your excess calories will rise that day. The last meal of the day should be as early as possible and as light as possible. This keeps that high point down and provides as little incentive as possible for the body to store calories as fat while you sleep.

Let's take a second look at that basic schedule shown earlier in this chapter. A person with an early afternoon activity peak might want to alter this schedule to look something like this:

MEAL	TIME	ENERGY AVAILABLE
FIRST BREAKFAST	7:00 A.M.	10:00 A.M.
SECOND BREAKFAST	9:00 A.M.	Noon
FIRST LUNCH	11:30 A.M.	2:30 P.M.
SECOND LUNCH	1:30 P.M.	4:30 P.M.
FIRST DINNER	6:00 P.M.	9:00 P.M.
SECOND DINNER	9:00 P.M.	Midnight.

A column has been added at the right to show the approximate time that the energy becomes available. The three hour lag is an approximation.

Use three hours in making up your schedule. Start right now. Make up a schedule of six meals a day. Later you can alter slightly depending on convenience. Set the times down now. Post them in a place where they will act as a reminder. If you have taken this step, you have begun the Miracle Diet. Happy, thinning days lie ahead.

> Mrs. I. Y. writes: "Losing weight on the Miracle Diet was a most rewarding experience. When you see the pounds disappearing, it brings back a state of reality to your mind. I can now remain on a diet without exerting too much effort. It is the best diet I have undertaken."

The Truth About "Quick Energy" Foods

About that three-hour approximation. Actually, carbohydrates take less time, while proteins and fats take longer.

That is why the makers of bread, cereals, and other carbohydrate foods can claim "quick energy" for their products. However, unless you are ready to expend energy that quickly, better think twice before selecting them to the exclusion of proteins and fats.

Protein comes closest to providing a steady conveyor belt flow of energy. It releases its energy into the bloodstream over a period of hours. Proteins from fish, poultry, meat, eggs, or vegetable sources differ in the actual time and people differ. But it is safe to say that protein deserves your special attention on the pages ahead if you are seeking to get as much weight loss mileage from your Miracle Diet.

SHE WAS A "CAKE-A-HOLIC"

Mrs. M. was in her early thirties. Her problem was a compulsion for cake. She would go on a bakery binge at least two or three times a week, buying an assortment of baked goods from as many as two or three shops at a time. Once the delectables were in her possession, she had no resistance. She ate them for breakfast, lunch and dinner, and in-between meals until the box or the bag was empty. Naturally, she had no desire to sit down with her family and eat at mealtimes and often made excuses for herself such as just not being hungry.

While of course gaining rapidly, she was losing the nourishment of a well-rounded diet and found herself constantly tired.

When Mrs. M. consulted me about her problem, she was 169 pounds. I patiently explained to her that no diet in the world included cake, although on a strict calorie diet it would be possible to include cake, but the expense of this inclusion would be phenomenal. For example, on a 1000 calorie diet, two pieces of cake would use up 700 of the available 1000 calories, leaving only 300 calories for the rest of the day's intake. Such a diet might read: Daily Intake—two pieces of cake and a medium hamburger.

Mrs. M. was a "cake-a-holic," the kind of person who could not eat small portions of cake, cookies, or sweets of any kind. She had to be weaned off cake completely. I used the 1200 Calorie Miracle Diet quite successfully, using the second, fourth and sixth meals as a "sweets" supplement, utilizing syrup packed fruit (without the syrup) and low calorie desserts fortified by skim milk and dried milk supplements (4 oz. skim milk and 1 heaping tablespoon of dried whole milk).

It is now three years later and Mrs. M. still buys cake for her family but no longer indulges. She is now one of the amateur tennis greats and tips the scale at a whispy 107 pounds.

The Miracle Diet is a balanced diet. But this may mean more proteins from animal and vegetable sources than you are now consuming. The average American diet is out of balance on the carbohydrate side.

Just the way six smaller meals reduce the peak of excess calories under three larger meals, six meals with emphasis on protein will flatter your excess calorie curve—and your excess bulges.

Vitamins and Minerals Add Health Not Calories

There are foods that are rich in vitamins and minerals and with no higher calorie count than foods that are depleted of these powerful nutrients. The fact is vitamins and minerals nourish the cell structure of the body without adding to blood sugar.

The Miracle Diet works its magic, not only by lessening the pressure to store excess calories, but also by lessening the body's demand for calories.

This demand for calories arises not necessarily from an energy deficiency, but it can arise just as easily from a nutrient deficiency.

Our stomach is not empty, but it says it is because the body craves certain structural materials.

This is not the same as false hunger. It is very real hunger. Perhaps even more real than when our stomach is empty and our body well nourished.

In a few reading minutes, you will be planning your six meals a day. You will be using your favorite foods selected from lists high in nutrients. You will be giving yourself liberal portions of valuable proteins in beef, veal, lamb, liver, pork and poultry. You will be choosing from over 25 kinds of fish, eggs, and cheeses.

You will be giving your body iron and calcium from molasses, fresh milk, liver, and bran cereal. You will be introduced to such miracle foods as wheat germ and yeast, and to such miracle vegetables as turnip greens and green peppers.

But the most satisfying miracle of all is that you will be able to set your quota and lose unwanted pounds just as fast and as much as you want.

With assured success.

Miracle Step Two

Set a basic schedule for your six-meal day. Time your first and second breakfasts, first and second lunches, first and second dinners. Fit them into your present office or family routine as closely as possible. Utilize a coffee break time, transform a snack time.

When you are used to six meals a day, you will then want to tailor the schedule in order to eat about three hours before periods of most activity. This will probably mean a shift to larger and earlier breakfasts, smaller and earlier dinners.

3

How to Make
the Pounds Roll Off

You have scheduled six meals a day. Now what do you eat for these meals?

I am going to put you on a strict 1200 calorie a day, six meals a day diet.

For most, it will bring a 1 percent weight loss a week. Two hundred pounders will lose two pounds a week, one hundred and fifty pounders will lose one and one half pounds a week.

Some will lose faster, some slower. But nobody will go hungry. In fact, it won't seem like you are on a diet at all.

The six meals, comprised of balanced nutrients, will quite likely feed your body better than you are feeding it now.

How Nature Helps Provide More Nutrients
in Fewer Calories

Over 2,000 years ago the ancient Greeks were striving for "a sound mind in a sound body" through proper diet and exercise. But even at that time the pressures of civilization were already forcing men away from the kind of natural eating that builds a sound person—mentally and physically.

Today civilization has come a long way, and so have our eating habits. But the latter way may not have been progress at all. No doubt about it, today's foods are more diversified thanks to modern transportation and refrigeration, but have we had to pay a price?

Yes, says Dr. Weston A. Price who recently made a survey of strong, healthy peoples of the world to see what their diets consisted of.[1] He learned that wherever he found people relatively free from disease, tooth decay, and other ailments, they were eating natural, fresh, pure, and unprocessed foods produced in their immediate environment.

In other words, for someone living on Long Island, N.Y., local potatoes and cabbage in the fall season would be more beneficial than Idaho potatoes and, perhaps, Georgia cabbage. The transportation that rushed these foods in from far away places may have been adding diversification but at the expense of more than money.

And the same might be true of freezing and other types of processing that civilization has developed.

Dr. Price has not been alone in his concepts. Nor free of disavowers. However, there has been no argument over whether fresh, organic, unprocessed, natural foods contain more vitamins, more minerals, more proteins, and more of the other nutrients and vital enzymes.

They do. By virtual consensus.

But nutrition experts disagree on whether the margin of advantage is really necessary or meaningful. Many believe that the minimum body requirements are quite adequately met by "civilized" foods with plenty of margin to spare—to go down the drain.

They may be right. But that argument does not apply when you are limiting intake to below daily calorie requirements.

On a 1200-calorie diet, there is a decided cutback in quantity of food. Not only is calorie intake below body requirements forcing fat to come out of storage and to be consumed, but nutrients are also quite likely to go below body requirements.

So we have to pick those foods that provide us with the most nutrients for the least calories.

---

[1] Paavo O. Airola, M.D., *There Is a Cure for Arthritis* (West Nyack, N.Y.: Parker Publishing Company, Inc., 1968).

Freshness provides an edge in nutrients per calorie over the same food preserved in any way.

This is particularly true of fruits and vegetables and many dairy products. Cooking, canning and freezing does not strip these foods of their nutritional value but it does reduce it. It surely does not increase it. And we are looking for every advantage per mouthful we can get. Freshness—epitomized by raw foods—is one of these advantages.

If your tastes or circumstances demand cooking, then cook as little as possible. Steaming is preferable, or cooking with very little water.

Freshness is a step closer to *living*. Living foods in natural conditions are nutritious foods. They are grown under natural conditions in man's own natural environment. It would be unnatural for an Eskimo to eat raw, natural papaya, just as it would be unnatural for a Polynesian to eat fresh, natural seal blubber.

In France, there is a company that operates a small ship that sails through that country's inland waterways on luxury gastronomic cruises. The menu is varied as the vessel reaches each area. In Champagne, the chicken is prepared with a champagne sauce instead of the usual white wine sauce. Oysters are on the table when sailing through Burgundy. Other dishes native to each area are placed on the menu as the vessel sails through.

This is a dramatic salute to the character and integrity of natural gastronomy. It says, in effect, that when in France eat like the French people do, and wherever you are in your own country, partake of your own area's food production with pride and enjoyment.

That is one element in the Miracle Diet.

How 1200 Calories Can Feel Like Overeating

The natural factor contributes not only to nutritional value but, because of this, to the satisfying quality of these foods. You do not get hungry on less food because, measured in terms of what your body craves, it may actually be more food, not less.

Another factor that should be taken into account is processing. Modern methods of food processing permit the food to go for weeks, possibly months, without deteriorating or spoiling. But if you were the manager of a health food shop—and there are thousands now all over the country—your biggest problem would be watching for mildew, worms, and other signs of spoilage. The "life" in unrefined foods is what invites attack by the scavengers of nature and by unwanted growths.

Refining foods often means taking out those materials in the food that are most "alive" and inserting chemicals that inhibit "life." White bread and white rice are foods that have been "refined." They are whiter, less coarse, more attractive, and less likely to spoil.

They are also more fattening per calorie and less nutritious per calorie. They have less bounce to the ounce.

What Different Types of Calories Can Do for You

When you eat 1200 calories a day of denatured, overly cooked foods that are heavy in sweets and starches, low in proteins, you can feel hungry all day and yet not lose weight.

You might even gain.

On the other hand, when you eat 1200 calories a day of natural, largely unprocessed foods rich in vitamins, minerals and proteins, you will never really feel hungry and yet you will lose weight.

How an Accountant Figured His Weight Loss

A 36-year-old accountant, who felt 20 years older and who was having trouble keeping his protruding paunch from eclipsing his books and records, decided to start his dieting on the 1200 calorie, six-meal-a-day regime that I will be giving you a few pages from now.

Six meals a day were easy for him. However, since he was to eat five of them in the corner luncheonette or local restaurant, he had some reservation as to whether he could obtain the precise foods that would give him the nutritional mileage the Miracle Diet sought.

I explained that the only absolutes about the Miracle Diet were the extension to six meals in a day and the limit to 1200 total calories in a day. The purpose of the other factors, I explained, were to make dieting easier on the body and on the morale. The more effort he put into tracking down the right foods, the less effort he would need to expand to stay on the diet.

This man really used ingenuity. He was a bachelor and able to spend time shopping and puttering around the kitchen. Breakfasts No. 1 and No. 2 were no problem. He took lunch No. 1 with him. Lunch No. 2 became a coffee break at the luncheonette and he enjoyed making dinner himself at home following simple recipes I gave him. In two weeks he had lost 3 percent of his weight —six pounds—"without wincing," as he put it.

He asked me to step him down to the 1000 calorie diet. "This is a joke," he complained, "let's bear down harder."

"You're losing fast enough," I replied, cautioning him that 1 percent per week was a safe rate at which to lose and he was already exceeding that.

Six weeks later, he had his wish. I shifted him from my 1200 calorie diet to the stiff 1000 calorie diet when his weight loss hit a plateau. He never noticed the difference. The last I saw him was 12 weeks after I met him. He stepped off the scales 31 pounds lighter and years younger.

Diets fail because people fail. If a diet is not easy for people to stay on, then it has the seeds within it for that failure.

Anybody can put together the semblance of a day's meals totaling 1000 calories and say, "Here, stay on this and you will lose weight." The catch is not in the promise you will lose weight. You will. The catch is in staying on the diet.

Some Fallacies About the Quantity of Food We Need

A recent survey at Cornell University showed that overeating is the major cause of aging in the developed countries of the world. Reporting on the study in the October 1965 issue of the *Canadian Medical Association Journal,* Dr. C. McCays writes that a scanty diet of nutritionally superior foods can add years to one's life.

Statistics collected in the Soviet Union show that one common characteristic of Russian centenarians is that they have all been moderate eaters.

Let me add one more truth to the world of knowledge about obesity:

> The more you eat today, the more it takes to satisfy you tomorrow.
>
> The less you eat today, the less you need to satisfy you tomorrow.

I know it's true. But I don't know why. I have my theories but I can't prove them.

For instance, as habit makers, we live by habits. If we are in the habit of eating a large dinner, we have a feeling of discontent until we fulfill that behavior pattern. It has nothing to do with "being full" as a matter of adequate nutrition.

Also, the habitual stretching of our stomach by a big meal conditions us to feel the need to keep eating until that stretched feeling "sounds the bell." Again, this has nothing to do with "being full."

Being full is satisfying the need to bring our blood sugar back up to par and the need to supply cellular building blocks for the renewal of our body—that endless life process.

You can do that with one fig. Or a few ounces of sautéed liver. Or a piece of camembert cheese.

If I could convince everyone in the first few minutes of conversation or reading that they were not hungry when they thought they were, I would have the key to solving America's greatest health hazard—obesity. But it is well-nigh impossible to dissuade a person that what he or she feels are not the pangs of hunger but rather the pangs of habit.

We need far less food than we think we need, and, if it's the right food, far less than even that.

One of the tricks that nature plays on us is to cause the same mental discomfort for real hunger as it does for habit unfulfilled. In both cases we experience irritability, fatigue, anxiety, depression and tension.

But one of the tricks *we* can play on nature is to eat foods of such high nutritious level that it prevents valid hunger and to eat so frequently that hunger symptoms—real or false—never have a chance to really "bug" us.

> Mrs. J. R. writes: "My blood pressure is normal. I have more energy. I have gained in self-confidence. I am less irritable. I find these six daily meals one of the easiest ways to lose weight. There is no battling to this diet and there are many side-benefits to be derived from it."

How little can we eat? People in countries that were considered suffering from food shortages in World War II were found to be in excellent health later. Shortage of food in general has never been the cause of starvation or disease. Shortage of a specific food, such as protein, or vitamin, or mineral, will certainly cause health problems.

Even people who have gone on fasts lasting ten or twenty days have emerged quite fit, energetic and robust after these experiences. Their body benefited more from the excess poundage it lost than from the temporary halt to vital nutrients.

The Pall of Malnutrition
That Plagues Even the Wealthy

Usually it's not how little we eat that gets us into trouble, it's what we eat. A National Nutrition Survey team recently visited ten states to pinpoint the extent of malnutrition in the world's richest nation. They found goiter, falling teeth, gums with gingivitis, skin problems, and stunted growth—all in pockets of deprivation, but almost equally existent in middle and even higher income areas.

It is common for physicians to find entire families suffering from symptoms of malnutrition in wealthy areas because doughnuts, cokes, popcorn, candy bars and coffee were replacing at least two of their three meals a day, and even the third was devoid of fruits or vegetables. "Why should I throw them out," one woman told me, "I just don't bother with them."

If births are outpacing world food production, then the problem is less a matter of quantity than it is of quality. We need to perfect not only the new rice and wheat varieties but ways of preparing them nutritiously, the wheat with its germ intact, the rice with its bran coating intact, or as much of it as possible. Humanity needs to reap not a larger quantity of food but a larger quantity of the three basic nutritional building blocks—riboflavin, niacin, and thiamin—and a larger quantity of all vitamins and minerals. These can be found in great quantity in small portions of the right foods.

We need to introduce the versatile soy bean into more countries so that they can reap its crop of protein. And we need to raise more vitamin C and vitamin D rather than just food.

Dr. Cortez F. Enloe Jr., editor and publisher of *Nutrition Today,* states that malnutrition affects the health of the rich and poor alike. He attributes this at least partially to the fact that the affluent are less dependent on staples such as bread which is now enriched, noting that products made with enriched flour have hit an all-time low. He believes that the poor and hungry are used "as foils" and that a depressed financial state is certainly not the only cause of malnutrition.

The Sweet Tooth Syndrome

If the eating habits of today's moderate income families skirt bread, it is probably because they are eating cake.

Sugar is, in my opinion, one of the greatest enemies of nutrition. Sugar is important in a diet—to a degree. But that degree has been far surpassed in this age of bottled soda, ice cream bars, doughnuts, cookies, cake, candy, sugared cereals, and pastry.

Sugar is 100 percent carbohydrate in its white, refined state—45 calories per tablespoonful. Brown sugar, when packed tight, is 51 calories per tablespoonful, 50 being carbohydrates and 1 calorie protein and vegetable fat due to the molasses.

People get hooked on sugar products. It probably starts when they are children and are offered sweets as a reward. They look on sweets as a festive moment. And who cannot look forward to the next one of those.

Actually, every moment spent in catering to the sweet tooth syndrome is a sad, not a festive, moment. For those sweets are far too loaded with calorie value for the body to cope with. If there is any food that turns on the fat forming and fat storing process fast, it is sugar.

I tell my clients who are hung up on sweets to start visualizing sweet food as turning to fat as soon as it enters their throat. It's an exaggeration but it helps to put sugar's taste in its true framework. Later I will give you some powerful mental tricks to break undesirable eating habits. Like that one.

The Basic Miracle Diet

I start all weight-losers on a 1200 calorie basic miracle diet. It is low in sweets, high in delicious, nutritious foods.

It provides six satisfying meals a day.

We try this diet for one week and then check the results. Not only do we measure the results on the scale, but the client expresses likes and dislikes regarding the specific foods and we make changes to satisfy those likes and dislikes.

I would like you to do the same.

Begin your weight loss by going on the Basic Miracle Diet timed according to the Basic Schedule or the revised schedule which you tailored to meet your daily activity schedule.

Let us examine this diet and see what makes it tick. For tick it does. It has ticked off thousands of pounds for hundreds of men and women, as regularly as clockwork.

Although there is a multitude of choices available, I will list a common selection that many seem to prefer and I will open the door of variety to you later.

Here are the six Basic Miracle Diet meals on a typical day.

BASIC (Weight Shaker) MIRACLE DIET—1200 Calories

BASIC TIME SCHEDULE	MEAL	MENU	PORTION
7 A.M.	BREAKFAST #1	Orange Juice	6 oz.
		Bran Cereal	¼ cup
		with milk	4 oz.
		and Wheat Germ	¼ tbs.
		and Molasses	1 tbs.
		Coffee, black	

Basic Time Schedule	Meal	Menu	Portion
10 A.M.	BREAKFAST #2	Tomato Juice	4 oz.
		Hardboiled egg	1 lg.
		Melba toast	2 sl.
1 P.M.	LUNCH #1	Vegetable Soup	¾ cup
		Saltine	1
		Coffee or tea	
4 P.M.	LUNCH #2	Regular Cottage Cheese	2 oz.
		with Pear Halves	2
7 P.M.	DINNER #1	Bouillon	1 cup
		Liver	4 oz.
		Boiled Potato	1 med.
		Cauliflower	4 oz.
		Cole Slaw	½ cup
		Skimmed Milk	8 oz. glass
		Coffee or tea	
10 P.M.	DINNER #2	Apple	1 med.
		Muenster Cheese	1 oz.

Remember this is just a typical day. This is not every day. Variety is essential in any diet and there are scores of substitutes for practically every item and therefore almost endless combinations.

It Feeds Not Just Your Stomach

Remember, too, that this is a diet that is richer than the average person's daily intake of protein, vitamins, minerals and essential nutrients.

It derives important protein from meats, organ meat, fish, poultry, cheese, soy beans and eggs.

It provides iron from bran cereal, molasses, and liver.

It bursts with vitamin A in parsley and other greens.

It is rich in vitamin B_1 via wheat germ, yeast, bran and pork.

It boasts liberal amounts of vitamin B_2 in liver, wheat germ and yeast.

It contains plenty of vitamin C in green peppers, parsley, broccoli, cauliflower, greens and fresh fruits.

It delivers niacin in bouillon cubes, yeast and bran in cereal.

It adds all of the other important essentials for a healthy, well-nourished body in its well-balanced six daily meals.

This Weight Shaker Diet Is 1200 Calories

I call this the Weight Shaker Miracle Diet. In all there are four levels of the Miracle Diet:

Weight Shaker Miracle Diet	Six meals 1200 calories
Weight Melter Miracle Diet	Six meals 1000 calories
Weight Dissolver Miracle Diet	Six meals 800 calories
Weight Blaster Miracle Diet	Six meals 600 calories

Those who begin the Miracle Diet customarily start with the Weight Shaker—1200-calorie—level. And they may never have to go any further.

This 1200-calorie regime may take their weight down at the desirable rate—1 percent of total weight per week—until they reach their right level.

This 1200-calorie level is less than half of the usual fare yet it will seem like no less eating. The nutritious food and the six meals contribute to a feeling of hunger satisfaction.

HOW A HOUSEWIFE REDUCED
From 213 to 135

Mrs. A. J. A., housewife, age 33, weighed 135 pounds when she was 22. She gained 5 pounds by age 23. Her weight increased to 175 pounds by age 28. At age 32, she weighed 196 pounds and when I first saw her, she weighed 213 pounds.

She always ate breakfast, mostly toast and tea. She usually ate lunch; when she did, it was a sandwich and she always ate dinner, mostly consisting of meat, vegetables, salad, and sometimes dessert. She did not normally eat between breakfast and lunch, but she ate between lunch and dinner, usually cake and coffee. She did not normally eat after dinner.

Her mother was overweight. Her father, sisters and brothers were of average weight. She occasionally bowled, swam in the summer and enjoyed horse-back riding.

When asked why she wanted to lose weight, she said, "To feel better and I'm tired of looking unattractive."

Using the 1200 calorie six-meal Miracle Diet, she easily returned to her 135 pound weight in six months. I was never tempted to cut her back even to the 1000 calorie Miracle Diet because she kept losing at least 1 percent of her weight week in and week out. She has now maintained her normal 135 pound weight and has regained her attractive appearance that goes with her normal or ideal weight.

Despite the 50 percent cut in calorie intake, many people will lose only for a short period of time. They seem to reach a plateau and need to cut calories even further in order to win back the losing streak.

That is why the four stages are often needed. Actually, you may find the results of the 1200-calorie Miracle Diet quite adequate. You may lose between one and three pounds a week all the way to your perfect slender figure.

I have occasionally seen a woman not lose at all on this 1200-calorie diet and have to cut further in order to get action.

Why does the poundage resist in this way? The reasons are the same as those we saw in Chapter 2 which resisted the pressure of excess calories in adding weight. The body does not lose fat at the drop of a calorie or store fat with the first excess calorie.

The body has its safety valves and its devices that resist the pressure of excess calories—for a time—and adjust to calorie shortages—for a time. This resistance must be overcome before weight changes occur.

The best way to overcome this resistance is to increase the pressure to take fat out of storage by making the calorie shortage more acute.

Even doctors are often fooled by this inertia of body weight. They cut their patients' calories 500 to 1000 a day and a week later nothing has happened. Naturally, they are inclined to blame it on cheating. This is a major reason why doctors are so often depressed at the lack of progress resulting from their advice on diet. A few admit that only about one patient in three shows any results.

Once the body begins to dump fat, the process continues. It is like trying to push a stalled car. Once you get it rolling, you can keep it rolling with much less effort.

This Weight Melter Miracle Diet
Is 1000 Calories Daily

To apply the calorie shortage pressure harder, the Weight Melter Miracle Diet slices the daily intake to 1000 calories.

You still eat six nutritious meals a day, as you can see below:

BASIC (Weight Melter) MIRACLE DIET—1000 Calories

BASIC TIME SCHEDULE	MEAL	MENU	PORTION
7 A.M.	BREAKFAST #1	Orange Juice	6 oz.
		Broiled Bacon	2 slices
		Coffee, black	1 cup
10 A.M.	BREAKFAST #2	Mushroom Omelette	1 egg
1 P.M.	LUNCH #1	Bouillon	1 cup
		Boiled Tongue	4 oz.
		Baked Potato	1 med.
		Salad, oil & vinegar dress.	½ cup
		Tea of Coffee	1 cup
4 P.M.	LUNCH #2	Molasses Milkshake	
		(Skimmed milk and	8 oz.
		molasses)	1 tbs.
7 P.M.	DINNER #1	Tomato Soup	¾ cup
		Broiled Codfish	4 oz. filet
		Boiled Cabbage	4 oz.
		Tea or Coffee	1 cup
10 P.M.	DINNER #2	Fresh strawberries	½ cup
		in	
		Skimmed Milk	1 oz.

You will see a number of foods repeated in this 1000-calorie diet which appeared in the 1200-calorie diet. This does not mean that there are no substitutes. Later we will provide you with equivalent foods and portions to build a variety of menus for each of the four Miracle Diets.

Of course, there are certain rich sources of nutrition which nature does not duplicate. Blackstrap molasses appears frequently in the diets as there is nothing quite like it. It is a by-product of the processing of white sugar and is rich in iron and in a long list of other minerals and nutrients.

Honey will be offered as another sweetener to choose for bran cereal or a spread. It has been called nature's perfect sweetener as it is one of the purest of foods. It contains vitamin C, thiamin, riboflavin and other B vitamins, digestive enzymes, amino acids, hormones and minerals.

You will see organ meats repeated. These are liver, sweetbreads, kidney, tongue, etc. They provide much more than just protein. You will see bran cereal repeated as cereal. It is the rice hulls which contain minerals and vitamins and roughage which acts to clean the system. All of this for less than 60 calories for a ¼ cup serving. By contrast most other prepared cereals have double the calorie value and much less nutritional value. A score of vital nutritive factors are removed from the whole grain and in their place are added chemicals and preservatives. Some makers add synthetic vitamins and iron, calling it enriched, but what has been taken out is far richer than what has been put in.

Certain fruits and vegetables will be favored because of their high nutritional value per calorie. Seeds and nuts will be offered as substitutes for those whose tastes they satisfy.

I WAS NEVER TEMPTED TO CHEAT

Leona T., unmarried, age 34, came to see me when she was 170 pounds. A year prior to this, she weighed approximately 150 pounds. She could look back when she weighed a desirable 127 pounds at the age of 27.

Her menu consisted of a cold cereal, two slices of bread, and several cups of coffee for breakfast. Lunch was usually a salad, a slice of bread, and coffee. Dinner was the standard meal consisting of meat, vegetables (mostly corn), potatoes, and a slice of bread, with coffee and cookies for dessert. Coffee-time, between each meal and after dinner, included a cookie snack. She ate for enjoyment and always felt a sense of con-tentment after eating.

Her father was the only exception to her normally weighted group of relatives.

Physically active, especially in the summer months, she was an avid swimmer, played tennis once a week, and enjoyed walking. The summer season offered her an opportunity "to take off a few pounds" as she put it. She bowled an average of 160 twice weekly during the winter.

When she came to me, she was depressed because she could not enjoy the new fashions in clothes, designed for the slim figure, and because she was being neglected by the opposite sex. Her indulgence in cookies and a starchy diet had certainly contributed to her condition of unattractiveness.

The 1200-Calorie Miracle Diet did not help her to reduce. However, she did reduce nicely on the 1000 Calorie Miracle Diet down to the 127 pounds she considered her most attrac-tive weight. She found she was not hungry on a 1000 daily calorie intake. "I was never tempted to cheat," she said. She now continues to enjoy her former svelteness. In her words, "I wouldn't change for anything."

I am going to let you glimpse the other two Miracle Diets now. You won't be starting these now. In fact, you may never have to use them at all as your weight may be "shaken" and "melted" to your normal youthful look by the 1200 or the 1000 calorie diets.

This Weight Dissolver Miracle Diet Is 800 Calories

Few dieters could take the normal 800 calorie diet that is generally prescribed. It is a starvation diet. But not this one. I will not say it does not take discipline to stay on it—it does. But it is not the form of torture that 800-calorie diets customarily cause. If you're fortunate, you may never even suffer a hunger pang while on it. The reason: six meals and plenty of solid nutrition.

WEIGHT DISSOLVER MIRACLE DIET—800 Calories

BASIC TIME SCHEDULE	MEAL	MENU	PORTION
7 A.M.	BREAKFAST #1	Bran Cereal	1 cup
		with milk	4 oz.
		and Wheat Germ	1 tbs.
		Coffee	1 cup
10 A.M.	BREAKFAST #2	Orange Juice	4 oz.
		Hard boiled egg	1 large
1 P.M.	LUNCH #1	Bouillon	1 cup
		Regular Cottage Cheese	4 oz.
		Sliced Chicken	2 oz.
		Tea or Coffee	1 cup
4 P.M.	LUNCH #2	Vanilla "Milkshake"	
		(Skim Milk	8 oz.
		Dried Milk	1 tbs.
		Vanilla)	3 drops
7 P.M.	DINNER #1	Boiled Shrimp	4 oz.
		Mixed Salad	½ cup
		Coffee	1 cup
10 P.M.	DINNER #2	Pineapple "Polynesia"	
		(Fresh pineapple	1 slice
		Honey)	1 tsp.

Here again, a number of "switches" and "trades" are available to suit the individual taste, and I will also provide you with ways to heighten the enjoyment with the use of calorie-free herbs and spices.

This Weight Smasher Miracle Diet Is 600 Calories

I want you to see this final—600 calorie—Miracle Diet, even though you will probably not have a chance to try it.

It's name is no dramatic gimmick. It literally smashes weight off a person when all else fails. It works its miracle without starvation, even though its calorie value is well below what is commonly held to be a starvation level.

However, you will know you are on a diet despite the six meals a day.

WEIGHT SMASHER MIRACLE DIET—600 Calories

BASIC TIME SCHEDULE	MEAL	MENU	PORTION
7 A.M.	BREAKFAST #1	Bran Cereal	¼ cup
		Wheat Germ	1 tbs.
		Milk	4 oz.
		Coffee	1 cup
10 A.M.	BREAKFAST #2	Orange Juice	4 oz.
1 P.M.	LUNCH #1	Bouillon	1 cup
		Hard Boiled Egg	1 large
		Tea or Coffee	1 cup
4 P.M.	LUNCH #2	Tomato Juice Cocktail	4 oz.
7 P.M.	DINNER #1	Broiled Calves Liver	4 oz.
		Mashed Turnips	½ cup
		Cole Slaw	½ cup
		Boiled Potato	½ med.
		Coffee or Tea	1 cup
10 P.M.	DINNER #2	Applesauce	¾ cup

In all of these four diets, I have done the calorie counting for you. All you have to do is select substitutes from the menus provided and which I will explain later.

If you are interested in how the Weight Smasher Miracle Diet manages to stay at the 600 calorie mark, here is the meal-by-meal tally:

BREAKFAST #1	127
BREAKFAST #2	64
LUNCH #1	87
LUNCH #2	30
DINNER #1	255
DINNER #2	40
TOTAL	603

SHE PREFERRED THE 600 CALORIE DIET
TO THE 1000 CALORIE DIET

Mrs. H. C. felt that she was overweight because of her feelings of aggression towards her husband. She was married at 19 and weighed less than 150 pounds. By the time she had reached her 21st birthday, her weight was at 200 pounds. Now, at 33 she sat tearfully in my office and weighed in at 241 pounds.

She normally ate two eggs for breakfast with toast and coffee. Her choice at lunch consisted of a couple of sandwiches or hamburgers with an accompanying coke. Her dinner, quite normal, consisted of meat, fish or poultry with a cooked vegetable. She informed me proudly that she never ate potatoes, but upon investigation, I found she ate cookies, cake and sandwiches galore between dinner and bed-time.

She had been on many diets but the longest she had ever "been a good girl," as she put it, was a three-week period in which she lost 6 pounds. She expressed her impatience at losing small amounts of weight and wanted to know how quickly she could lose weight.

I started her on the 600 calorie—Six-Meal Miracle Diet—with astonishing rewards. In the first month, she had lost 35 pounds. When I informed her physician, he was somewhat apprehensive about this weight loss and persuaded me to increase her intake to 1000 calories.

However, Mrs. H. C. wasn't too pleased with this new arrangement. She convinced her physician to allow her to stay on the 600 Calorie Diet. She won. She did stay on the 600 Calorie Diet all the seven months it took to reach 138 pounds.

She now maintains her weight on the 1200-Calorie Diet. I first put her on the 1500-Calorie Diet for maintenance but she began to gain weight. However, the 1200-Calorie Diet has been perfect for her.

In the next chapter, we will create some interesting menus from a variety of valuable foods which nature provides. Some will mean new and exciting dining for you. Others will be "old faithfuls" dressed up in new flavors.

All will be brimming with nutrients that will revitalize your body as you slenderize.

Miracle Step Three

If you wish, get your physician's permission to go on one of the four six-meal-a-day diets: 1200, 1000, 800, or 600 calories. You may want to start on the 1200-calorie diet first and shift down until your weight loss is significant. That is, 1½ pounds per week for a 150 pound person; 2 pounds per week for a 200 pound person, etc. but do not exceed a loss of 1 percent of your weight per week.

4

Thirty Days of
Varied Miracle Menus

"Follow this diet. Make no substitutions. See me next week." A woman is handed a typewritten slip. There are three meals listed for each of three days. There are three more items in invisible ink: taste boredom, taste hunger, diet failure.

We all crave taste experiences. Most diets place us in a taste prison. And, like any prisoner, we immediately begin to look for a means to escape to taste freedom.

Since we are all voluntary dieters, escape from a taste prison is easy. We just quit the diet. Some do it frankly and openly "I'll begin seriously next week . . . next month . . . after the holidays." Others nibble, snack, and switch. "Doctor, I can't understand it. There must be something wrong with the scale."

We are not to blame. The diet is to blame.

It is totally unrealistic to place a human being in a civilized environment bursting with taste sensations and say: "Don't." It would be different if that person were marooned on a deserted island and at the point of starvation caught a sea turtle. Given a choice of surviving or not surviving, a monotonous fare can be sheer paradise.

But surrounded by bulging supermarkets, arm's reach refrigerators, and gourmet restaurants, it can be agonizing to live with an arbitrary, harsh reducing diet.

80

A Tasty Dish for Every Palate

The Miracle Diet would never work if it did not satisfy our natural craving for a variety of flavors, tastes, textures, and temperatures.

In Bali, in the South Pacific, the food is always abundantly flavored with a variety of crushed, pungent spices. Cooking always involves nuts, onions, grated coconut, fermented fish paste, aromatic roots and leaves—and a liberal measure of burning red peppers. Even Balinese babies are fed this peppery food as soon as they are weaned.

Needless to say, Balinese food is an "ordeal by fire" to the average westerner. To the Balinese, however, their food is delicious and American or European food is "nyam-nyam" (flat and tasteless).

Incidentally, the Balinese are always nibbling. They frequent public eating booths where they can buy a piece of roast chicken for a dime or a package of rice for a penny or two. Street vendors sell snacks wrapped in banana leaf. Their meals are at odd hours. There is usually only one formal daily meal and this is quite modest, even frugal.

Shades of the Miracle Diet! Are the Balinese fat because of constant eating? On the contrary. They are slim, lithe and among the most handsome and beautiful people on earth.

The point is that tastes differ widely and to succeed, the Miracle Diet must satisfy all tastes. You don't have to travel to the South Pacific to find people who like spicy food and people who like bland food. They all live within a block of each other.

On the pages ahead, I have listed menus for thirty days of varied, interesting dining—six meals for each day. I have done this for the four different Miracle Diet levels—1200 calories, 1000 calories, 800 calories and 600 calories. In some cases a meal may be the same for all four diets, but since you are on only one of them at a time, you still enjoy thirty different days.

How to Use the 30-Day Menus

I must admit that some foods listed in these menus are not exactly what you might expect to find on Mr. and Mrs. Jones's breakfast table or even in one in a hundred kitchens. Nevertheless, you are invited to be more adventurous in your dining and to try some ideas that may never have crossed your shopping path before. Let the Miracle Diet add variety to your usual everyday dining habits, instead of adding restrictions to it.

Restriction insures failure. Variety invites success.

This does not mean that just because the 20th day of the 600-calorie diet calls for a second breakfast consisting of blackberry juice, you must find blackberry juice. No, you can repeat any of the other juices you have already found to your liking or you can look ahead to the next ten days and select another.

REMEMBER THIS:

All 30 days are interchangeable. That is, you may substitute Breakfast #1 on one day for Breakfast #1 on any other day (same calorie level). You will still have the correct calorie count and a well-balanced nutritional day.

Similarly, you can substitute one Dinner #2 for another Dinner #2 (same calorie level) or change any Lunch #1 for another Lunch #1.

Substitutions may be by day only.

You may not substitute from a different calorie level, that is by shifting from 1200 to 1000 or vice versa. You may not substitute one kind of a meal for another like breakfast for lunch or lunch for dinner. You may not substitute a #1 for a #2 or vice versa.

But you can thumb through the days, if you wish and select a different day for a particular meal. Make your taste buds happy.

Substitutions may also be made on similar items within a meal. If you don't have the time to make French toast in the morning, certainly you can substitute any of the cereals listed for other days.

If you care not for salmon steak, but the rest of the meal is to your liking, substitute another meat or fish, swordfish or baked ham.

Anyone caught eliminating an entree and substituting a second dessert gets suspended from the club.

Start with the 1200-Calorie Miracle Diet

Everybody starts with the 1200-calorie Miracle Diet.

There are no exceptions.

You shift to the next lower calorie level—1000—only when your rate of loss slows down before you have reached your goal.

You may have to shift several times. Some may eventually reach the 600-calorie diet to insure continued loss until normal weight is reached.

I am going to make it easy for you to know if and when you should shift to a lower gear. Here is a table of probable weight loss for those on any of the four different calorie level diets. It also shows a "too slow" weight loss. When you hit the "too slow" weight loss, it is time for a change. You may want to check with your physician and keep him advised of your progress and of any intent to change to a lower calorie-level Miracle Diet.

CALORIE LEVEL CHANGER CHART

(Start on the 1200-calorie Miracle Diet. Change to the 1000 only if weight loss is less than that shown in the right hand column. Use the chart later to determine if you should next shift to the 800-calorie Miracle Diet and later again to determine if you should shift to the 600-calorie Miracle Diet.)

Your Present Weight	Satisfactory Weekly Weight Loss	Time to Shift if Weekly Weight Loss Drops Below
110 to 125 pounds	½ to 1 pound	½ pound
125 to 150 pounds	1 to 1 ½ pounds	1 pound
150 to 175 pounds	1 ½ to 1 ¾ pounds	1 ½ pounds
175 to 200 pounds	1 ¾ to 2 pounds	1 ¾ pounds
200 to 225 pounds	2 to 2 ½ pounds	2 pounds
225 to 250 pounds	2 ½ to 3 pounds	2 ½ pounds
over 250 pounds	3 or more pounds	3 pounds

Now you are ready to turn the page and start Day Number One. Use the right hand column—the 1200-calorie Miracle Diet. Stay with it seven days. Then if your weight loss is not satisfactory according to the above table, move one column to the left and you will be on the 1000-calorie Miracle Diet—still six wholesome meals a day. Even if you have to make such a column shift three times and you wind up on the 600-calorie Miracle Diet, you will still enjoy six meals a day with a different fare every day.

Good luck! And good eating!

MIRACLE DIET MENUS

Special Note: Tea may be had with lemon, coffee must be black.

600 Calorie

Breakfast No. 1
1 poached egg
Coffee or tea

Breakfast No. 2
Apple juice (4 oz.)

Lunch No. 1
Grilled cheese—1 slice bread plus 1 tbs. grated cheese
Coffee or tea

Lunch No. 2
Clam cocktail (4 oz. jar)

Dinner No. 1
Open sandwich—Avocado
1 slice whole wheat bread
Coffee or tea

Dinner No. 2
½ cantaloupe

800 Calorie

Breakfast No. 1
½ cup orange juice, frozen, (diluted)
1 med. egg (soft, poached or scrambled)
1 rye crisp (double square)
Coffee or tea

Breakfast No. 2
1 slice toast, garlic (French bread)
½ cup chicken broth

Lunch No. 1
½ cup soup, pepperpot or chicken-rice
2 slices bacon, broiled
1 med. tomato
1 large gingersnap cookie
Coffee or tea

Lunch No. 2
½ cup chicken rice or pepperpot soup
1 med. fresh plum

Dinner No. 1
Ground round, broiled (3 oz.)
1 cup summer squash, boiled
½ cup cauliflower, cooked or 2 slices tomato
Coffee or tea

Dinner No. 2
Any No. 2 meal on the 600-Calorie Diet

1000 Calorie

Breakfast No. 1
Pineapple-orange juice (4 oz.) frozen, diluted (Dole)
Oatmeal (4 oz.)
Skim milk (4 oz.)
3 rye or wheat thins
Coffee or tea

Breakfast No. 2
Same as 800-Calorie Diet

Lunch No. 1
1 salmon steak, baked
1 tsp. lemon juice
1 piece Zweibach toast or ½ med. apple
Coffee or tea

Lunch No. 2
Same as 800-Calorie Diet

Dinner No. 1
Bass, baked (5 oz.)
12 large fresh mushrooms broiled or
½ cup brussels sprouts, cooked
Coffee or tea

Dinner No. 2
Any No. 2 meal on the 600-Calorie Diet

1200 Calorie

Breakfast No. 1
½ cup orange juice
2 egg omelet (plain)
2 rye crisps (double square)
Coffee or tea

Breakfast No. 2
Same as 800-Calorie Diet

Lunch No. 1
Lean roast beef (6 oz.)
½ cup cooked fresh peas
1 med. cucumber, slices
Coffee or tea

Lunch No. 2
Same as 800-Calorie Diet

Dinner No. 1
1 cup tomato juice
3 slices turkey (white meat)
1 cup spinach, cooked
Coffee or tea

Dinner No. 2
Any No. 2 meal on the 600-Calorie Diet

MIRACLE DIET MENUS

DAY TWO

600 Calorie

Breakfast No. 1
Cottage cheese (2 oz.)
Coffee or tea

Breakfast No. 2
Apricot nectar (4 oz.)

Lunch No. 1
2 slices bacon
Coffee or tea

Lunch No. 2
3 oz. Crab, canned

Dinner No. 1
Cottage cheese and pickles
Coffee or tea

Dinner No. 2
2 oz. cottage cheese with
1 slice tangerine

800 Calorie

Breakfast No. 1
¼ cantaloupe
1 med. egg (soft, poached or scrambled)
½ cup skim milk
Coffee or tea

Breakfast No. 2
2/3 banana, sliced, large

Lunch No. 1
¾ cup soup, clear chicken
2–3 slices smoked salmon, small
1 slice toast, light rye or whole wheat
½ tsp. butter
Coffee or tea

Lunch No. 2
½ med. apple or
1 nectarine
1 large celery stalk
4 rye or wheat thins

Dinner No. 1
1 cup cantaloupe (diced)
1 ave. chicken leg, roasted
12 large mushrooms, broiled
½ med. potato, baked
Coffee or tea

Dinner No. 2
Any No. 2 meal on the 600-Calorie Diet

1000 Calorie

Breakfast No. 1
½ cup pineapple in juice, chunks or crushed (Dole)
1 med. egg, poached
1 slice toast, whole wheat
Coffee or tea

Breakfast No. 2
Same as 800-Calorie Diet

Lunch No. 1
1/3 cup cottage cheese (creamed)
1 large Romaine leaf
6 med. scallops, broiled
6 large fresh mushrooms, broiled
or
½ cup cauliflower, cooked
Coffee or tea

Lunch No. 2
Same as 800-Calorie Diet

Dinner No. 1
2 soft-shell crabs, fried
½ cup brusselssprouts, cooked
or
1 med. tomato
Coffee or tea

Dinner No. 2
Any No. 2 meal on the 600-Calorie Diet

1200 Calorie

Breakfast No. 1
½ grapefruit, small
1 tsp. sugar
2 eggs (poached, or soft)
3 rye or wheat thins
Coffee or tea

Breakfast No. 2
Same as 800-Calorie Diet

Lunch No. 1
½ cup soup, pepperpot
Roast beef, lean (6 oz.)
1 cup cauliflower, cooked
Coffee or tea

Lunch No. 2
Same as 800-Calorie Diet

Dinner No. 1
3 med. slices brisket of beef
½ med. potato, boiled
2 large celery stalks
Coffee or tea

Dinner No. 2
Any No. 2 meal on the 600-Calorie Diet

MIRACLE DIET MENUS

DAY THREE

600 Calorie

Breakfast No. 1
¼ cup bran cereal
Skim milk (4 oz.)
Coffee or tea

Breakfast No. 2
Grape juice (4 oz.)

Lunch No. 1
Slice Vienna beef (2 oz.)
Coffee or tea

Lunch No. 2
Crab cocktail (4 oz.)

Dinner No. 1
2 med. eggs
Coffee or tea

Dinner No. 2
4 stewed prunes

800 Calorie

Breakfast No. 1
½ med. orange sliced
1 med. egg
1 piece Zweibach toast
Coffee or tea

Breakfast No. 2
1 cup tomato juice
4 tsp. cottage cheese, creamed

Lunch No. 1
1 cup consommé
1 small Romaine leaf
5 tbs. tuna salad
2 tsp. cottage cheese, creamed
½ cup banana whip pudding
Coffee or tea

Lunch No. 2
⅔ cup fresh strawberries
2 tsp. sour cream
2 rye or wheat thins

Dinner No. 1
½ cup soup, pepperpot or
   chicken-rice
Calf's liver, broiled (3 oz.)
1 cup summer squash, boiled
Coffee or tea

Dinner No. 2
Any No. 2 meal on the 600-
   Calorie Diet

1000 Calorie

Breakfast No. 1
½ pkg. melon balls, frozen
8 oz. cup yogurt, plain
Coffee or tea

Breakfast No. 2
Same as 800-Calorie Diet

Lunch No. 1
10 clams, fried
Coffee or tea

Lunch No. 2
Same as 800-Calorie Diet

Dinner No. 1
Halibut steak, broiled (5 oz.)
⅔ cup brussel sprouts, cooked
Coffee or tea

Dinner No. 2
Any No. 2 meal on the 600-
   Calorie Diet

1200 Calorie

Breakfast No. 1
½ cup tomato juice
1 med. orange, sliced
1 slice French toast
1 tbs. maple syrup
Coffee or tea

Breakfast No. 2
Same as 800-Calorie Diet

Lunch No. 1
½ cup V-8 juice
Lean roast beef (6 oz.)
1 cup cauliflower, cooked
   or
1 med. tomato
Coffee or tea

Lunch No. 2
Same as 800-Calorie Diet

Dinner No. 1
½ cup soup, noodle
Lean leg of lamb, roasted (5 oz.)
1 cup cooked spinach
½ cup banana whip pudding
Coffee or tea

Dinner No. 2
Any No. 2 meal on the 600-
   Calorie Diet

87

MIRACLE DIET MENUS

DAY FOUR

600 Calorie	800 Calorie	1000 Calorie	1200 Calorie
Breakfast No. 1	*Breakfast No. 1*	*Breakfast No. 1*	*Breakfast No. 1*
White fish (2 oz.)	¼ cantaloupe	Tangerine juice (4 oz.) frozen	1 whole med. orange
Coffee or tea	½ English muffin or bagel	reconstituted	2 slices toast, light rye or whole
	½ tsp. grape jelly	½ cup cooked oatmeal	wheat
	½ cup puffed wheat (unsweetened)	2/3 cup skim milk	2 tsp. orange marmalade or
	1/3 cup skim milk	2/3 tsp. sugar	strawberry jam
	Coffee or tea	Coffee or tea	1/3 cup skim milk
			Coffee or tea
Breakfast No. 2	*Breakfast No. 2*	*Breakfast No. 2*	*Breakfast No. 2*
Orange juice (4 oz.)	4 tsp. cottage cheese, creamed	Same as 800-Calorie Diet	Same as 800-Calorie Diet
	1 slice toast, light rye		
Lunch No. 1	*Lunch No. 1*	*Lunch No. 1*	*Lunch No. 1*
1 slice liver sausage	½ cup soup, all vegetable	2 large celery stalks	1 cup consommé
Coffee or tea	½ cup cottage cheese, creamed	1 med. deviled crab	Salmon steak, broiled (4 oz.)
	1 large Romaine leaf	½ med. potato, baked	1 tbs. lemon juice
	2 sugar wafer cookies	Coffee or tea	½ cup white rice, cooked
	Coffee or tea		Coffee or tea
Lunch No. 2	*Lunch No. 2*	*Lunch No. 2*	*Lunch No. 2*
Gefilte fish, 1 piece	½ cup fruit flavored gelatin	Same as 800-Calorie Diet	Same as 800-Calorie Diet
Dinner No. 1	*Dinner No. 1*	*Dinner No. 1*	*Dinner No. 1*
Lettuce and tomato	½ cup soup, lentil	Swordfish steak, broiled (5 oz.)	2 large celery stalks
Coffee or tea	1 ave. chicken leg, roasted	¾ cup beets, cooked	Ground round (6 oz.)
	½ med. potato, baked	Coffee or tea	1 med. potato, boiled
	Coffee or tea		Coffee or tea
Dinner No. 2	*Dinner No. 2*	*Dinner No. 2*	*Dinner No. 2*
3 cheese crackers with cheese filling	Any No. 2 meal on the 600-Calorie Diet	Any No. 2 meal on the 600-Calorie Diet	Any No. 2 meal on the 600-Calorie Diet

MIRACLE DIET MENUS

600 Calorie	*800 Calorie*	*1000 Calorie*	*1200 Calorie*
Breakfast No. 1	*Breakfast No. 1*	*Breakfast No. 1*	*Breakfast No. 1*
Wheaties (4 oz.)	1 slice toast, light rye or whole wheat	½ cup orange juice, frozen diluted	1 cup oatmeal, cooked
Skim milk (4 oz.)	½ tsp. grape jelly	3 slices bacon, broiled	1 cup skim milk
Coffee or tea	1 tsp. cream cheese	Coffee or tea	1 tsp. sugar
	½ cup puffed rice		Coffee or tea
	1/3 cup skim milk		
	½ tsp. sugar		
	Coffee or tea		
Breakfast No. 2	*Breakfast No. 2*	*Breakfast No. 2*	*Breakfast No. 2*
Grapefruit juice (4 oz.)	2 med. cheese crackers	Same as 800-Calorie Diet	Same as 800-Calorie Diet
	1 tbs. bacon-cheese spread		
Lunch No. 1	*Lunch No. 1*	*Lunch No. 1*	*Lunch No. 1*
3 slices ham, cured	1 cup consommé	5 tbs. tuna salad	1 cup fresh pineapple, diced
Coffee or tea	1 saltine cracker	½ cup brown rice, cooked	1 slice toast, light rye or whole wheat
	Fillet of sole, broiled (6 oz.)	1 cup pickled beets	1 tsp. grape jelly
	½ cup pickled beets	1 carrot (strips)	6 tbs. creamed cottage cheese
	Coffee or tea	1 large celery stalk	½ cup caramel pudding
		Coffee or tea	Coffee or tea
Lunch No. 2	*Lunch No. 2*	*Lunch No. 2*	*Lunch No. 2*
1 piece of white fish and pickle	1 carrot (strips)	Same as 800-Calorie Diet	Same as 800-Calorie Diet
	1 slice toast, rye or whole wheat		
Dinner No. 1	*Dinner No. 1*	*Dinner No. 1*	*Dinner No. 1*
Tuna (½ individual can)	1 slice baked ham *or*	1 cup beef-vegetable stew	Ground round (6 oz.)
	1 slice corned beef	½ cup skim milk	½ cup brown rice, cooked
	½ med. potato, baked	Coffee or tea	¾ cup broccoli, cooked
	1 cup green beans, cooked		Coffee or tea
	1 rye crisp (double square)		
	Coffee or tea		
Dinner No. 2	*Dinner No. 2*	*Dinner No. 2*	*Dinner No. 2*
½ grapefruit	Any No. 2 meal on the 600-Calorie Diet	Any No. 2 meal on the 600-Calorie Diet	Any No. 2 meal on the 600-Calorie Diet

MIRACLE DIET MENUS

DAY SIX

600 Calorie

Breakfast No. 1
¼ cup 40 percent bran
Skim milk (4 oz.)
Coffee or tea

Breakfast No. 2
Orange juice (4 oz.)

Lunch No. 1
3 links sausage ham
Coffee or tea

Lunch No. 2
Pickled herring (3 oz.)

Dinner No. 1
Grated cheese (2 tbs.)
Coffee or tea

Dinner No. 2
Tangerines (4)

800 Calorie

Breakfast No. 1
¼ cantaloupe
¾ cup puffed wheat (unsweetened)
2/3 cup skim milk
1 tsp. sugar
1 rye crisp (double square)
Coffee or tea

Breakfast No. 2
½ cup applesauce, canned (unsweetened)

Lunch No. 1
1 med. tomato
1 cup oyster stew (skim milk)
1 saltine cracker
Coffee or tea

Lunch No. 2
1 cup fresh pineapple, diced

Dinner No. 1
1 cup cantaloupe, diced
½ ave. chicken breast, roasted
1 cup mashed turnips sprinkled with ginger
Coffee or tea

Dinner No. 2
Any No. 2 meal on the 600-Calorie Diet

1000 Calorie

Breakfast No. 1
Orange-grapefruit juice (4 oz.) frozen, reconstituted
1 cup puffed wheat (unsweetened)
1 cup skim milk
2 crackers, onion flavored
Coffee or tea

Breakfast No. 2
Same as 800-Calorie Diet

Lunch No. 1
¼ cup tomato juice
¾ canned lobster meat
1 cup spinach, cooked
½ mashed potatoes (w/milk)
2/3 cup sauerkraut
Coffee or tea

Lunch No. 2
Same as 800-Calorie Diet

Dinner No. 1
Veal cutlet, broiled (4 oz.)
1 cup pickled beets
Coffee or tea

Dinner No. 2
Any No. 2 meal on the 600-Calorie Diet

1200 Calorie

Breakfast No. 1
½ med. orange, sliced
1 cup corn flakes
1 cup skim milk
2 tsp. sugar
Coffee or tea

Breakfast No. 2
Same as 800-Calorie Diet

Lunch No. 1
½ cup soup, pepperpot
10 clams, fried
Coffee or tea

Lunch No. 2
Same as 800-Calorie Diet

Dinner No. 1
¾ cup tomato juice
1 cup consommé
1 cup beef and vegetable stew
1 slice white bread
1 tsp. butter
Coffee or tea

Dinner No. 2
Any No. 2 meal on the 600-Calorie Diet

MIRACLE DIET MENUS

DAY SEVEN

600 Calorie

Breakfast No. 1

1 egg, boiled
Coffee or tea

Breakfast No. 2

Peach nectar (4 oz.)

Lunch No. 1

3 slices turkey, pressed
Coffee or tea

Lunch No. 2

Shrimp in cocktail sauce
 (4 oz. jar)

Dinner No. 1

Minced ham (1 heaping tbs.)
Coffee or tea

Dinner No. 2

1 slice fresh pineapple 1" thick

800 Calorie

Breakfast No. 1

½ med. orange, sliced
1 med. egg
4 rye or wheat thins
Coffee or tea

Breakfast No. 2

1 med. nectarine
½ cup skim milk

Lunch No. 1

1 cup soup, onion
3 oz. smoked white fish
Coffee or tea

Lunch No. 2

1 slice white toast
½ tsp. butter

Dinner No. 1

1 med. lean veal chop, braised
½ cup wax beans, cooked
Coffee or tea

Dinner No. 2

Any No. 2 meal on the 600-
 Calorie Diet

1000 Calorie

Breakfast No. 1

1 cup wheat flake cereal
1 cup skim milk
¼ tsp. sugar
Coffee or tea

Breakfast No. 2

Same as 800-Calorie Diet

Lunch No. 1

6 med. fresh shrimp, boiled
1 tsp. lemon
1 med. ear of corn
1 tsp. butter
½ cup fresh peas, cooked
1 large celery stalk
Coffee or tea

Lunch No. 2

Same as 800-Calorie Diet

Dinner No. 1

Beef, boiled (4 oz.)
½ med. potato, baked
Coffee or tea

Dinner No. 2

Any No. 2 meal on the 600-
 Calorie Diet

1200 Calorie

Breakfast No. 1

1 med. tangerine
1 cup wheat flake cereal
1 cup skim milk
1 tsp. sugar
Coffee or tea

Breakfast No. 2

Same as 800-Calorie Diet

Lunch No. 1

1 salmon steak, baked
2 tsp. lemon juice
1 med. egg (soft, poached or
 hard)
1 celery stalk
1 rye or wheat thin
Coffee or tea

Lunch No. 2

Same as 800-Calorie Diet

Dinner No. 1

½ cup V-8 juice
1 cup beef and vegetable stew
½ cup banana whip pudding
1 sugar wafer cookie
Coffee or tea

Dinner No. 2

Any No. 2 meal on the 600-
 Calorie Diet

MIRACLE DIET MENUS

DAY EIGHT

600 Calorie

Breakfast No. 1
Pot cheese (2 oz.)
Coffee or tea

Breakfast No. 2
Pineapple juice (4 oz.)

Lunch No. 1
Mixed green salad (8 oz.)
Coffee or tea

Lunch No. 2
1 tbs. anchovie paste
2 saltine crackers

Dinner No. 1
1 slice chicken
Coffee or tea

Dinner No. 2
1 cup consommé

800 Calorie

Breakfast No. 1
½ med. orange, sliced
¾ cup puffed wheat (unsweetened)
2/3 cup skim milk
½ tsp. sugar
Coffee or tea

Breakfast No. 2
½ cup V-8 juice
3 rye or wheat thins

Lunch No. 1
1 cup consommé
Kippered herring (3 oz.)
1 large celery stalk
5 cucumber slices
Coffee or tea

Lunch No. 2
½ cup fresh strawberries
½ cup skim milk

Dinner No. 1
1 med. fresh plum *or*
1 cup cantaloupe, diced
Roast beef (4 oz.)
2 slices tomato
Coffee or tea

Dinner No. 2
Any No. 2 meal on the 600-Calorie Diet

1000 Calorie

Breakfast No. 1
¼ cup tomato juice
½ cup fresh cherries
1 med. egg (soft or hard cooked)
1 slice toast, rye or whole wheat
1 tsp. grape jelly
Coffee or tea

Breakfast No. 2
Same as 800-Calorie Diet

Lunch No. 1
2 slices white turkey meat
or
2 slices corned beef
½ med. potato, baked or boiled
Coffee or tea

Lunch No. 2
Same as 800-Calorie Diet

Dinner No. 1
Sirloin steak, broiled (4 oz.)
1 cup wax beans, cooked
Coffee or tea

Dinner No. 2
Any No. 2 meal on the 600-Calorie Diet

1200 Calorie

Breakfast No. 1
½ cup orange juice, frozen
1 English muffin
2 tsp. grape jelly or strawberry jam or orange marmalade
1/3 cup skim milk
Coffee or milk

Breakfast No. 2
Same as 800-Calorie Diet

Lunch No. 1
1 salmon steak, baked
2 tsp. lemon juice
½ med. potato, baked
½ cup skim milk
Coffee or tea

Lunch No. 2
Same as 800-Calorie Diet

Dinner No. 1
½ cup fresh fruit salad
1 cup Hungarian goulash
Coffee or tea

Dinner No. 2
Any No. 2 meal on the 600-Calorie Diet

MIRACLE DIET MENUS

DAY NINE

	600 Calorie	800 Calorie	1000 Calorie	1200 Calorie
Breakfast No. 1	Wheat stacks (4 oz.) Skim milk (4 oz.) Coffee or tea	½ cup orange juice, frozen diluted ½ cup corn flakes 1/3 cup skim milk ½ tsp. sugar ½ rye crisp (double square) Coffee or tea	1 cup tomato juice ½ waffle ½ tsp. butter 1 tsp. maple syrup Coffee or tea	¼ cantaloupe 2 eggs (poached, soft-cooked) 1 slice toast, light rye or whole wheat 1 tsp. grape jelly Coffee or tea
Breakfast No. 2	Pear nectar (4 oz.)	¾ cup tomato juice 1 piece Zwieback toast	Same as 800-Calorie Diet	Same as 800-Calorie Diet
Lunch No. 1	Egg salad (1 egg, lettuce and tomato) Coffee or tea	½ cup soup, noodle or barley ¾ cup lobster meat, canned 1 large celery stalk 1 piece Zwieback toast Coffee or tea	Chicken livers, broiled (4 oz.) 1 cup spinach, cooked 3 cookies, chocolate snap Coffee or tea	10 clams, fried 1 med. tomato 2 rye or wheat thins Coffee or tea
Lunch No. 2	Cottage cheese (3 oz.)	1 cup consommé or 4 radishes 2 saltines with 2 tsp. guava butter	Same as 800-Calorie Diet	Same as 800 Calorie Diet
Dinner No. 1	1 slice turkey Coffee or tea	1 cup oyster stew with skim milk 10 tiny oyster crackers Coffee or tea	Lean leg of lamb, roasted (5 oz.) ¾ cup broccoli, cooked Coffee or tea	Corned beef hash (3 ½ oz.) 1 med. potato, baked with ½ tbs. melted butter 1 large celery stalk 1 cup junket Coffee or tea
Dinner No. 2	Cottage cheese, plain (3 oz.)	Any No. 2 meal on the 600-Calorie Diet	Any No. 2 meal on the 600-Calorie Diet	Any No. 2 meal on the 600-Calorie Diet

MIRACLE DIET MENUS

600 Calorie	800 Calorie	1000 Calorie	1200 Calorie
Breakfast No. 1	*Breakfast No. 1*	*Breakfast No. 1*	*Breakfast No. 1*
¼ cup bran with raisins	½ cup orange juice, frozen, diluted	¾ cup tomato juice	½ med. banana
Skim milk (4 oz.)	1 buckwheat pancake (4" diameter)	*or*	1 egg, poached or soft-cooked
Coffee or tea	¼ tsp. butter	1 med. tangerine	1 slice Canadian bacon, broiled
	1 tsp. maple syrup	1 med. English muffin or bagel	1 slice toast, light rye or whole wheat
	¼ cantaloupe	1 tsp. butter	1 tsp. grape jelly
	Coffee or tea	Coffee or tea	Coffee or tea
Breakfast No. 2	*Breakfast No. 2*	*Breakfast No. 2*	*Breakfast No. 2*
Pineapple-grapefruit juice (4 oz.)	½ med. apple or orange or nectarine	Same as 800-Calorie Diet	Same as 800-Calorie Diet
	4 tsp. creamed cottage cheese		
Lunch No. 1	*Lunch No. 1*	*Lunch No. 1*	*Lunch No. 1*
Lobster salad	½ cup soup, chicken rice	Ground round steak, broiled (5 oz.)	1 cup fresh pineapple, diced
(½ cup lobster, mixed green salad)	6 asparagus spears	½ cup cauliflower, cooked	Chicken livers, broiled (4 oz.)
Coffee or tea	1 slice bologna on 1 slice whole wheat bread	Coffee or tea	½ cup apple snow pudding
	½ med. banana		Coffee or tea
	Coffee or tea		
Lunch No. 2	*Lunch No. 2*	*Lunch No. 2*	*Lunch No. 2*
Buttermilk (8 oz.)	1 slice fresh pineapple	Same as 800-Calorie Diet	Same as 800-Calorie Diet
2 saltine crackers	3 rye or wheat thins		
Dinner No. 1	*Dinner No. 1*	*Dinner No. 1*	*Dinner No. 1*
Grilled tomato	1 slice baked ham *or*	Calf's liver, broiled (7 oz.)	Flank steak, broiled, sliced (4 oz.)
Coffee or tea	1 slice corned beef *or*	½ cup zucchini, cooked	2/3 cup pickled beets
	3 ave. chicken wings, roasted	Coffee or tea	Coffee or tea
	½ cup carrots, cooked, diced		
	½ med. potato, baked		
	1/3 cup skim milk		
	Coffee or tea		
Dinner No. 2	*Dinner No. 2*	*Dinner No. 2*	*Dinner No. 2*
1 cup strawberries	Any No. 2 meal on the 600-Calorie Diet	Any No. 2 meal on the 600-Calorie Diet	Any No. 2 meal on the 600-Calorie Diet

MIRACLE DIET MENUS

600 Calorie	800 Calorie	1000 Calorie	1200 Calorie
Breakfast No. 1	*Breakfast No. 1*	*Breakfast No. 1*	*Breakfast No. 1*
1 shirred egg Coffee or tea	½ med. fresh peach, sliced 2/3 cup corn flakes ¾ tsp. sugar ½ cup skim milk Coffee or tea	1 med. muffin, bran or corn 1 tsp. butter 2/3 cup skim milk Coffee or tea	½ cup canned applesauce (unsweetened) 1 med. egg atop 1 English muffin 1 slice Canadian bacon Coffee or tea
Breakfast No. 2	*Breakfast No. 2*	*Breakfast No. 2*	*Breakfast No. 2*
Tangerine juice (4 oz.)	1 slice Holland Rusk toast 4 tsp. creamed cottage cheese	Same as 800-Calorie Diet	Same as 800-Calorie Diet
Lunch No. 1	*Lunch No. 1*	*Lunch No. 1*	*Lunch No. 1*
Shrimp salad (½ cup shrimp, mixed green salad) Coffee or tea	½ cup V-8 juice ¾ cup lobster meat, canned 2 tsp. lemon juice, 1 tsp. caper 4 small radishes 12 tiny cheese tid-bit crackers 3 large celery stalks Coffee or tea	Calf's liver, broiled (6 oz.) 4 radishes *or* 2 large celery stalks Coffee or tea	¼ cup tomato juice Chicken livers, broiled (4 oz.) 1 med. egg (hard, or soft) 1 slice bacon, broiled Coffee or tea
Lunch No. 2	*Lunch No. 2*	*Lunch No. 2*	*Lunch No. 2*
¼ cup cottage cheese with vegetable salad	1 tbs. cream cheese 2 rye or wheat thins	Same as 800-Calorie Diet	Same as 800-Calorie Diet
Dinner No. 1	*Dinner No. 1*	*Dinner No. 1*	*Dinner No. 1*
Anchovies (5) Coffee or tea	2-egg omelet (cooked in ½ tbs. butter) Coffee or tea	Ground round (6 oz.) 1 large celery stalk Coffee or tea	Sirloin steak, broiled (4 oz.) 1 cup spinach, cooked 1 med. potato, boiled 1 large celery stalk Coffee or tea
Dinner No. 2	*Dinner No. 2*	*Dinner No. 2*	*Dinner No. 2*
2 oz. creamed cottage cheese	Any No. 2 meal on the 600-Calorie Diet	Any No. 2 meal on the 600-Calorie Diet	Any No. 2 meal on the 600-Calorie Diet

MIRACLE DIET MENUS

DAY TWELVE

600 Calorie

Breakfast No. 1
Asparagus omelet (1 egg)
Coffee or tea

Breakfast No. 2
Pineapple-orange juice (4 oz.)

Lunch No. 1
3 fresh oysters
Coffee or tea

Lunch No. 2
1 tbs. chicken paste
2 saltine crackers

Dinner No. 1
Cucumber and watercress
Coffee or tea

Dinner No. 2
1 orange

800 Calorie

Breakfast No. 1
1/3 cup fresh grapefruit sections
1/2 cup oatmeal, cooked
1/2 cup skim milk
1/2 tsp. sugar
Coffee or tea

Breakfast No. 2
1/2 cup tomato juice
1/2 slice Swiss cheese

Lunch No. 1
1/2 cup Manhattan clam chowder
1/2 waffle
1/2 tsp. melted butter
1/2 tbs. maple syrup
6 cucumber slices *or*
1 large celery stalk
Coffee or tea

Lunch No. 2
1/2 slice cheese, Swiss or American
2 saltine crackers

Dinner No. 1
1/2 cup soup, chicken vegetable
Ground round steak, broiled (3 oz.)
5 artichoke hearts, canned
Coffee or tea

Dinner No. 2
Any No. 2 meal on the 600-Calorie Diet

1000 Calorie

Breakfast No. 1
1/2 med. orange, sliced
2 slices toast, rye or whole wheat
1 tsp. jelly
1 tsp. butter
Coffee or tea

Breakfast No. 2
Same as 800-Calorie Diet

Lunch No. 1
2 lean lamb shops, broiled (loin)
1 med. tomato
Coffee or tea

Lunch No. 2
Same as 800-Calorie Diet

Dinner No. 1
3 slices boiled ham
Coffee or tea

Dinner No. 2
Any No. 2 meal on the 600-Calorie Diet

1200 Calorie

Breakfast No. 1
1/2 cup pineapple in juice (chunks or crushed)
2/3 cup bran
1 tsp. sugar
1 cup skim milk
Coffee or tea

Breakfast No. 2
Same as 800-Calorie Diet

Lunch No. 1
1/2 cup V-8 juice
1 slice baked ham *or* corned beef
2 slices tomato
1/2 med. potato, baked
1/2 cup banana whipped pudding
Coffee or tea

Lunch No. 2
Same as 800-Calorie Diet

Dinner No. 1
Sirloin steak, broiled (4 oz.)
1/2 cup brown rice, cooked
1/2 cup gelatin, fruit flavor
Coffee or tea

Dinner No. 2
Any No. 2 meal on the 600-Calorie Diet

MIRACLE DIET MENUS

DAY THIRTEEN

600 Calorie

Breakfast No. 1
Farmer cheese (2 oz.)
Coffee or tea

Breakfast No. 2
Cranberry juice (4 oz.)

Lunch No. 1
Chicken, sliced (2 oz.)
Coffee or tea

Lunch No. 2
¼ cup cottage cheese
with vegetable salad

Dinner No. 1
Egg salad (1 egg) with chopped
cucumber
Coffee or tea

Dinner No. 2
1 cup raspberries

800 Calorie

Breakfast No. 1
½ small grapefruit
1 tsp. sugar
1 med. egg
½ saltine
Coffee or tea

Breakfast No. 2
½ canned peach
1 piece Zweibach toast

Lunch No. 1
¾ cup soup, clear chicken
Chicken livers, broiled (4 oz.)
Coffee or tea

Lunch No. 2
2/3 cup skim milk
1 large gingersnap cookie *or*
2 rye or wheat thins

Dinner No. 1
1 slice corned beef *or*
3 ave. chicken wings, roasted *or*
1 slice baked ham
1 med. potato, baked
Coffee or tea

Dinner No. 2
Any No. 2 meal on the 600-
Calorie Diet

1000 Calorie

Breakfast No. 1
2/3 cup tomato juice
2-egg omelet (plain)
Coffee or tea

Breakfast No. 2
Same as 800 Calorie Diet

Lunch No. 1
3 ave. chicken wings, roasted
1 med. potato, boiled
1 cup broccoli, cooked
Coffee or tea

Lunch No. 2
Same as 800-Calorie Diet

Dinner No. 1
3 slices turkey (white meat)
Coffee or tea

Dinner No. 2
Any No. 2 meal on the 600-
Calorie Diet

1200 Calorie

Breakfast No. 1
1 cup fresh pineapple, diced
2 slices bacon, broiled
1 med. egg (soft, poached or hard)
Coffee or tea

Breakfast No. 2
Same as 800-Calorie Diet

Lunch No. 1
2 slices turkey (white meat)
1 cup pickled beets
½ cup skim milk
Coffee or tea

Lunch No. 2
Same as 800-Calorie Diet

Dinner No. 1
Sirloin steak, broiled (4 oz.)
2/3 brussels sprouts cooked
½ cup junket
Coffee or tea

Dinner No. 2
Any No. 2 meal on the 600-
Calorie Diet

97

MIRACLE DIET MENUS

DAY FOURTEEN

600 Calorie	800 Calorie	1000 Calorie	1200 Calorie
Breakfast No. 1 2 slices Canadian bacon Coffee or tea	*Breakfast No. 1* ½ cup fresh strawberries 1 tsp. sugar ½ cup skim milk 1 slice toast, light rye or whole wheat ½ tsp. butter Coffee or tea	*Breakfast No. 1* 1 med. egg (scrambled) 2 slices melba toast ½ pkg. melon balls, frozen Coffee or tea	*Breakfast No. 1* ¼ cantaloupe 1 slice ham, baked or boiled 1 slice rye toast 1 tsp. grape jelly 2/3 cup skim milk Coffee or tea
Breakfast No. 2 Lemonade (4 oz.)	*Breakfast No. 2* ½ med. tomato sliced 4 tsp. creamed cottage cheese ½ cup skim milk	*Breakfast No. 2* Same as 800-Calorie Diet	*Breakfast No. 2* Same as 800-Calorie Diet
Lunch No. 1 Beef liver, broiled 3/8" thick Coffee or tea	*Lunch No. 1* ½ cup soup, chicken rice 3 slices bacon, broiled 6 cucumber slices *or* 1 large celery stalk Coffee or tea	*Lunch No. 1* Swordfish steak, broiled (5 oz.) Coffee or tea	*Lunch No. 1* ¼ cantaloupe Swordfish steak (5 oz.) 2 tsp. lemon juice ½ cup zucchini, cooked 1 rye or wheat thin Coffee or tea
Lunch No. 2 Skim milk (8 oz.) 2 saltine crackers	*Lunch No. 2* 1 oz. Camembert cheese	*Lunch No. 2* Same as 800-Calorie Diet	*Lunch No. 2* Same as 800-Calorie Diet
Dinner No. 1 Shrimp salad (3 oz.) with chopped celery Coffee or tea	*Dinner No. 1* 1 large frankfurter (all beef) 1 cup broccoli, cooked Coffee or tea	*Dinner No. 1* Lean roast beef (6 oz.) 1 cup spinach, cooked 2 sugar wafer cookies Coffee or tea	*Dinner No. 1* 1 cup bouillon 3 slices baked ham 6 asparagus spears 1 med. tomato 1 med. fresh peach, sliced
Dinner No. 2 1 pear	*Dinner No. 2* Any No. 2 meal on the 600-Calorie Diet	*Dinner No. 2* Any No. 2 meal on the 600-Calorie Diet	*Dinner No. 2* Any No. 2 meal on the 600-Calorie Diet

MIRACLE DIET MENUS

DAY FIFTEEN

600 Calorie	800 Calorie	1000 Calorie	1200 Calorie
Breakfast No. 1 Oat cereal (4 oz.) Skim milk (4 oz.) Coffee or tea	**Breakfast No. 1** ½ canned pear ½ cup strawberry Yogurt Coffee or tea	**Breakfast No. 1** 2/3 cup bran flakes 1 cup skim milk 2 tsp. sugar Coffee or tea	**Breakfast No. 1** ½ pkg. melon balls, frozen 1 cup Yogurt, vanilla or coffee Coffee or tea
Breakfast No. 2 Pink Lemonade (4 oz.)	**Breakfast No. 2** ½ cup fresh strawberries 4 tsp. sour cream	**Breakfast No. 2** Same as 800-Calorie Diet	**Breakfast No. 2** Same as 800-Calorie Diet
Lunch No. 1 Pike, canned (4 oz.) Coffee or tea	**Lunch No. 1** 1 cup consomme' Chicken livers, broiled (4 oz.) 2 large celery stalks 12 tiny cheese crackers Coffee or tea	**Lunch No. 1** 2 slices meat loaf (ground round) 2 slices tomato Coffee or tea	**Lunch No. 1** 1 cup tomato juice 1 tongue sandwich on 2 slices rye 1 tsp. mustard Coffee or tea
Lunch No. 2 3 oz. pot cheese	**Lunch No. 2** ½ cup soup, noodle or barley 1 saltine cracker	**Lunch No. 2** Same as 800-Calorie Diet	**Lunch No. 2** Same as 800-Calorie Diet
Dinner No. 1 Lobster salad (3 oz.) with chopped pepper Coffee or tea	**Dinner No. 1** ½ canned peach 1 slice meat loaf (with ground round) 1 cup spinach, cooked Coffee or tea	**Dinner No. 1** ¼ cup soup, chicken vegetable ½ cup diced chip beef, creamed on 1 slice white bread Coffee or tea	**Dinner No. 1** 3 slices corned beef 1 cup spinach, cooked 2/3 cup skim milk Coffee or tea
Dinner No. 2 ¾ cup Loganberries	**Dinner No. 2** Any No. 2 meal on the 600-Calorie Diet	**Dinner No. 2** Any No. 2 meal on the 600-Calorie Diet	**Dinner No. 2** Any No. 2 meal on the 600-Calorie Diet

MIRACLE DIET MENUS

DAY SIXTEEN

600 Calorie	800 Calorie	1000 Calorie	1200 Calorie
Breakfast No. 1	*Breakfast No. 1*	*Breakfast No. 1*	*Breakfast No. 1*
Mushroom omelet (1 egg)	½ med. fresh peach, sliced	1 cup cantaloupe, diced *or*	Melon balls, frozen
Coffee or tea	1 med. egg	1 med. fresh plum	2 slices smoked salmon
	1 slice toast, light rye or whole wheat	1 cup corn flakes	½ cup Yogurt, plain or coffee
	Coffee or tea	1 cup skim milk	Coffee or tea
		2 tsp. sugar	
		Coffee or tea	
Breakfast No. 2	*Breakfast No. 2*	*Breakfast No. 2*	*Breakfast No. 2*
Fruit punch (4 oz.)	1 cup soup, onion	Same as 800-Calorie Diet	Same as 800-Calorie Diet
	2 large celery stalks		
Lunch No. 1	*Lunch No. 1*	*Lunch No. 1*	*Lunch No. 1*
Cottage cheese, (3 oz.)	½ cup soup, all-vegetable	1 cup beef and vegetable stew	¼ honeydew melon
Coffee or tea	1 slice corned beef	Coffee or tea	1 tongue sandwich on 2 slices rye
	½ tsp. mustard		1 tsp. mustard
	1 slice rye or whole wheat bread		Coffee or tea
	Coffee or tea		
Lunch No. 2	*Lunch No. 2*	*Lunch No. 2*	*Lunch No. 2*
1 cup soup, vegetable	½ cup soup, barley	Same as 800-Calorie Diet	Same as 800-Calorie Diet
	1 whole wheat biscuit		
Dinner No. 1	*Dinner No. 1*	*Dinner No. 1*	*Dinner No. 1*
½ cup Sweetbreads, veal	1 slice meat loaf (ground round)	¼ cup soup, chicken vegetable	10 clams, fried
Coffee or tea	½ cup mashed potatoes (w/milk)	*or*	1 med. potato, boiled with ½ tbs. melted butter
	4 radishes *or*	½ cup brusselssprouts, cooked	Coffee or tea
	2 large celery stalks	7 oz. lean pot roast	
	Coffee or tea	Coffee or tea	
Dinner No. 2	*Dinner No. 2*	*Dinner No. 2*	*Dinner No. 2*
4 plums	Any No. 2 meal on the 600-Calorie Diet	Any No. 2 meal on the 600-Calorie Diet	Any No. 2 meal on the 600-Calorie Diet

MIRACLE DIET MENUS

DAY SEVENTEEN

600 Calorie	800 Calorie	1000 Calorie	1200 Calorie
Breakfast No. 1 ¼ cup bran with raisins Coffee or tea	*Breakfast No. 1* 1 small orange, sliced 1 slice toast, whole wheat 1 tsp. grape jelly *or* ½ tsp. butter 1/3 cup skim milk Coffee or tea	*Breakfast No. 1* 1 small orange, sliced 1 buckwheat pancake (4" diameter) ½ tsp. butter 1 tsp. maple syrup 2/3 cup skim milk Coffee or tea	*Breakfast No. 1* 2 slices smoked salmon 1 bagel or English muffin 1 tsp. butter Coffee or tea
Breakfast No. 2 Sauerkraut juice (4 oz.)	*Breakfast No. 2* 1 cup soup, onion 1 saltine cracker	*Breakfast No. 2* Same as 800-Calorie Diet	*Breakfast No. 2* Same as 800-Calorie Diet
Lunch No. 1 Haddock, smoked (4 oz.) Coffee or tea	*Lunch No. 1* ¼ cup tomato juice 1 med. deviled crab Coffee or tea	*Lunch No. 1* 1 cup oyster stew (with skim milk) 1 cup mashed turnips 3 sugar wafer cookies Coffee or tea	*Lunch No. 1* 1 cup beef vegetable stew ¼ honeydew melon Coffee or tea
Lunch No. 2 1 tbs. liver pate 2 soda crackers	*Lunch No. 2* 1 carrot (strips) ½ cup skim milk 1 saltine cracker	*Lunch No. 2* Same as 800-Calorie Diet	*Lunch No. 2* Same as 800-Calorie Diet
Dinner No. 1 Crabmeat salad (3 oz.) Coffee or tea	*Dinner No. 1* 3 ½ oz. corned beef hash 1 cup cooked spinach ½ cup cauliflower, cooked *or* ½ med. tomato, sliced Coffee or tea	*Dinner No. 1* 2 small lean pork chops, broiled 1 slice eggplant, fried (½" thick) *or* 1 cup spinach, cooked Coffee or tea	*Dinner No. 1* 3 med. slices leg of veal, roasted 1 med. ear of corn ½ cup skim milk Coffee or tea
Dinner No. 2 3 oz. pot cheese	*Dinner No. 2* Any No. 2 meal on the 600-Calorie Diet	*Dinner No. 2* Any No. 2 meal on the 600-Calorie Diet	*Dinner No. 2* Any No. 2 meal on the 600-Calorie Diet

MIRACLE DIET MENUS

DAY EIGHTEEN

600 Calorie

Breakfast No. 1
Smoked salmon (1 oz.)
Coffee or tea

Breakfast No. 2
Strawberry juice (4 oz.)

Lunch No. 1
Calf's liver, broiled (3/8" thick)
Coffee or tea

Lunch No. 2
¼ cup cottage cheese with chives

Dinner No. 1
Kidney, veal—1 whole
Coffee or tea

Dinner No. 2
Grapes (4 oz.)

800 Calorie

Breakfast No. 1
1 medium tangerine
½ cup Yogurt, strawberry
Coffee or tea

Breakfast No. 2
1 cup soup, onion
10 tiny cheese crackers

Lunch No. 1
½ cup tomato juice
6 med. scallops, baked
1 tsp. lemon juice
6 asparagus spears
Coffee or tea

Lunch No. 2
2 tbs. creamed cottage cheese
2 rye crisp (double square)

Dinner No. 1
½ cup chicken broth
Calf's liver, broiled (3 oz.)
5 canned artichoke hearts
½ cup stewed tomatoes
1 large celery stalk
Coffee or tea

Dinner No. 2
Any No. 2 meal on the 600-Calorie Diet

1000 Calorie

Breakfast No. 1
1 med. fresh peach, sliced
1 slice French toast
1 tsp. maple syrup
Coffee or tea

Breakfast No. 2
Same as 800-Calorie Diet

Lunch No. 1
¼ cup soup, chicken vegetable
1 cup Yogurt, strawberry
Coffee or tea

Lunch No. 2
Same as 800-Calorie Diet

Dinner No. 1
¼ cup soup, chicken vegetable
3 slices bacon, broiled
½ med. potato, baked or boiled
2 sugar wafer cookies
Coffee or tea

Dinner No. 2
Any No. 2 meal on the 600-Calorie Diet

1200 Calorie

Breakfast No. 1
¼ cup tomato juice
1 medium banana
2 slices smoked salmon
2/3 cup skim milk
Coffee or tea

Breakfast No. 2
Same as 800-Calorie Diet

Lunch No. 1
½ cup carrot juice
Calf's liver, broiled (6 oz.)
2 tbs. creamed cottage cheese
Coffee or tea

Lunch No. 2
Same as 800-Calorie Diet

Dinner No. 1
½ cup mashed potatoes (with milk)
Veal cutlet, broiled (4 oz.)
1 cup spinach, cooked
1 med. fresh peach
Coffee or tea

Dinner No. 2
Any No. 2 meal on the 600-Calorie Diet

MIRACLE DIET MENUS

600 Calorie

Breakfast No. 1
Cream of wheat (4 oz.)
Skim milk (4 oz.)
Coffee or tea

Breakfast No. 2
Blueberry juice (4 oz.)

Lunch No. 1
1 slice Swiss cheese
Coffee or tea

Lunch No. 2
1 cup tomato soup

Dinner No. 1
1 tbs. paté de foie gras
2 soda crackers
Coffee or tea

Dinner No. 2
1 cup bouillon, hot or cold

800 Calorie

Breakfast No. 1
1 slice fresh pineapple
1 med. egg
1/3 cup skim milk
Coffee or tea

Breakfast No. 2
2/3 cup barley soup

Lunch No. 1
¼ cup tomato juice   or
½ cup sauerkraut juice
1 slice baked ham
2/3 large banana, sliced
Coffee or tea

Lunch No. 2
½ cup fresh raspberries
½ cup skim milk

Dinner No. 1
½ cup stewed tomatoes
2 ave. chicken legs, broiled
Coffee or tea

Dinner No. 2
Any No. 2 meal on the 600-Calorie Diet

1000 Calorie

Breakfast No. 1
1 medium banana
1 cup skim milk
1 tsp. sugar
Coffee or tea

Breakfast No. 2
Same as 800-Calorie Diet

Lunch No. 1
½ cup Yogurt, strawberry
1 oz. Camembert cheese
2/3 cup fresh blackberries
Coffee or tea

Lunch No. 2
Same as 800-Calorie Diet

Dinner No. 1
½ cup chicken salad
½ cup broccoli, cooked
½ cup fruit flavored gelatin
Coffee or tea

Dinner No. 2
Any No. 2 meal on the 600-Calorie Diet

1200 Calorie

Breakfast No. 1
½ cup orange juice, frozen, diluted
1 medium banana
2 slices Canadian bacon, broiled
Coffee or tea

Breakfast No. 2
Same as 800-Calorie Diet

Lunch No. 1
Calf's liver, broiled (6 oz.)
1 cup green beans, cooked
½ medium apple
Coffee or tea

Lunch No. 2
Same as 800-Calorie Diet

Dinner No. 1
½ cup soup, noodle
1 ave. chicken breast, roasted
1 cup green beans, cooked
½ medium banana
½ cup skim milk
Coffee or tea

Dinner No. 2
Any No. 2 meal on the 600-Calorie Diet

103

MIRACLE DIET MENUS

DAY TWENTY

600 Calorie

Breakfast No. 1
¼ cup bran with wheat germ
Skim milk (4 oz.)
Coffee or tea

Breakfast No. 2
Blackberry juice (4 oz.)

Lunch No. 1
Stuffed tomato with 2 oz. crabmeat
Coffee or tea

Lunch No. 2
3 oz. farmer cheese

Dinner No. 1
2 slices boiled ham (1/8" thick)
Coffee or tea

Dinner No. 2
1 cup gooseberries

800 Calorie

Breakfast No. 1
¼ med. honeydew melon
½ cup Yogurt, vanilla or coffee
½ tsp. sugar
Coffee or tea

Breakfast No. 2
¾ cup Manhattan clam chowder
10 tiny cheese crackers

Lunch No. 1
1 cup consomme
1 slice baked ham
4 radishes or 2 celery stalks
½ cup fresh strawberries with 2 tbs. skim milk
1 tsp. sugar
1 large romaine leaf
4 tsp. creamed cottage cheese
Coffee or tea

Lunch No. 2
½ cup carrot juice
½ slice American cheese (small *or* ½ slice Swiss cheese

Dinner No. 1
Chicken livers, broiled (4 oz.)
¾ cup broccoli, cooked
Coffee or tea

Dinner No. 2
Any No. 2 meal on the 600-Calorie Diet

1000 Calorie

Breakfast No. 1
2 slices bacon, broiled
1 med. egg (poached, soft-cooked or hard)
2 rye or wheat thins
Coffee or tea

Breakfast No. 2
Same as 800-Calorie Diet

Lunch No. 1
½ medium apple
2 ave. size chicken legs, broiled
¾ cup diced carrots, cooked
Coffee or tea

Lunch No. 2
Same as 800-Calorie Diet

Dinner No. 1
2-egg cheese omelet
2 large celery stalks
Coffee or tea

Dinner No. 2
Any No. 2 meal on the 600-Calorie Diet

1200 Calorie

Breakfast No. 1
2 medium fresh plums
1 slice baked ham
½ cup Yogurt, plain or coffee
Coffee or tea

Breakfast No. 2
Same as 800-Calorie Diet

Lunch No. 1
2 soft shell crabs, fried
1 medium tomato
2 celery stalks
Coffee or tea

Lunch No. 2
Same as 800-Calorie Diet

Dinner No. 1
1 salmon steak, baked
1 med. potato, baked with ½ tbs. melted butter
½ cup skim milk
1 large celery stalk
Coffee or tea

Dinner No. 2
Any No. 2 meal on the 600-Calorie Diet

MIRACLE DIET MENUS

600 Calorie

Breakfast No. 1

Tomato omelet (1 egg)
Coffee or tea

Breakfast No. 2

Red Currant juice (4 oz.)

Lunch No. 1

Camembert cheese (1" arc)
Coffee or tea

Lunch No. 2

1 cup soup, chicken

Dinner No. 1

Beef liver, broiled
(3/8" thick)
Coffee or tea

Dinner No. 2

3 crackers with cheese
filling

800 Calorie

Breakfast No. 1

½ cup fresh blueberries
1/3 cup skim milk
½ tsp. sugar
Coffee or tea

Breakfast No. 2

½ cup soup, all-vegetable
10 tiny Oyster crackers

Lunch No. 1

½ cup soup, all-vegetable
1 large frankfurter (all beef)
1 tsp. mustard
Coffee or tea

Lunch No. 2

½ med. egg (hard-cooked)
½ glass skim milk

Dinner No. 1

1 slice meat loaf
(with ground round)
½ cup white rice, cooked
Coffee or tea

Dinner No. 2

Any No. 2 meal on the 600-
Calorie Diet

1000 Calorie

Breakfast No. 1

¼ cantaloupe
1 bagel *or* English muffin
½ slice American cheese
Coffee or tea

Breakfast No. 2

Same as 800-Calorie Diet

Lunch No. 1

1 frankfurter (all beef)
½ cup sauerkraut
½ cup fruit flavored gelatin
Coffee or tea

Lunch No. 2

Same as 800-Calorie Diet

Dinner No. 1

½ cup tomato-aspic salad
1 cup Yogurt, strawberry
6 asparagus spears
1 large celery stalk
Coffee or tea

Dinner No. 2

Any No. 2 meal on the 600-
Calorie Diet

1200 Calorie

Breakfast No. 1

2 eggs (poached or soft-cooked
or hard)
2 slices smoked salmon
Coffee or tea

Breakfast No. 2

Same as 800-Calorie Diet

Lunch No. 1

1 cup consommé
2 soft shell crabs, fried
1 medium fresh plum
Coffee or tea

Lunch No. 2

Same as 800-Calorie Diet

Dinner No. 1

½ med. orange, sliced
1 cup Manhattan clam chowder
2-egg omelet
3 slices bacon
Coffee or tea

Dinner No. 2

Any No. 2 meal on the 600-
Calorie Diet

MIRACLE DIET MENUS

DAY TWENTY-TWO

600 Calorie

Breakfast No. 1

1 slice bologna
Coffee or tea

Breakfast No. 2

Tomato juice (4 oz.)

Lunch No. 1

Turkey, sliced (2 oz.)
Coffee or tea

Lunch No. 2

4 cubes cheddar cheese
2 soda crackers

Dinner No. 1

Calf's liver, broiled
(3/8" slice)
Coffee or tea

Dinner No. 2

2 oz. cottage cheese with 2 guavas

800 Calorie

Breakfast No. 1

½ cup tomato juice
1 medium egg
1 piece Zweibach toast
¼ tsp. butter
Coffee or tea

Breakfast No. 2

½ cup soup, pepperpot or
   chicken-rice
2 saltine crackers

Lunch No. 1

1 cup cantaloupe, diced *or*
   1 med. fresh plum
1 large frankfurter (all beef)
1 tsp. mustard
2 large celery stalks *or*
   1 cup consommé
Coffee or tea

Lunch No. 2

1 medium egg (poached, soft-
   cooked or hard)

Dinner No. 1

½ cup white rice, cooked
3 ave. chicken wings, roasted
2 slices tomato *or*
   ½ cup cauliflower, cooked
Coffee or tea

Dinner No. 2

Any No. 2 meal on the 600-
   Calorie Diet

1000 Calorie

Breakfast No. 1

½ cup orange juice, frozen
   diluted
2 slices Canadian bacon, broiled
½ slice toast, white
Coffee or tea

Breakfast No. 2

Same as 800-Calorie Diet

Lunch No. 1

½ cup chicken salad
2 slices tomato
2 med. cheese crackers
Coffee or tea

Lunch No. 2

Same as 800-Calorie Diet

Dinner No. 1

1 med. serving Welsh rabbit on
   toast
½ cup skim milk
2 sugar wafer cookies
Coffee or tea

Dinner No. 2

Any No. 2 meal on the 600-
   Calorie Diet

1200 Calorie

Breakfast No. 1

2/3 med. orange, sliced
2 eggs
1 slice smoked salmon
Coffee or tea

Breakfast No. 2

Same as 800-Calorie Diet

Lunch No. 1

1 medium nectarine
½ cup soup, chicken rice
1 cup Yogurt, strawberry
Coffee or tea

Lunch No. 2

Same as 800-Calorie Diet

Dinner No. 1

½ cup soup, barley
1 ave. breast of chicken, roasted
½ cup brown rice, cooked
1 cup tomatoes, stewed
Coffee or tea

Dinner No. 2

Any No. 2 meal on the 600-
   Calorie Diet

MIRACLE DIET MENUS

600 Calorie

Breakfast No. 1
Bran cereal (4 oz.)
Skim milk (4 oz.)
Coffee or tea

Breakfast No. 2
Raspberry juice (4 oz.)

Lunch No. 1
Fruit salad (peach, plum, ½ cup strawberries)
Coffee or tea

Lunch No. 2
1 cup soup, chicken gumbo

Dinner No. 1
Heart (lamb), 1 oz. (2" long)
Coffee or tea

Dinner No. 2
1 cup consommé, hot or cold

800 Calorie

Breakfast No. 1
½ medium banana
½ cup puffed rice
2/3 cup skim milk
1 tsp. sugar
Coffee or tea

Breakfast No. 2
½ cup soup, lentil
1 saltine cracker

Lunch No. 1
¼ cantaloupe
1 large romaine leaf
½ cup creamed cottage cheese
1 cup consommé or 4 radishes
4 rye or wheat thins
Coffee or tea

Lunch No. 2
½ med. tomato, sliced
1 whole wheat biscuit
½ cup skim milk

Dinner No. 1
Lean roast beef (4 oz.)
½ cup green beans, cooked
1 medium fresh peach
Coffee or tea

Dinner No. 2
Any No. 2 meal on the 600-Calorie Diet

1000 Calorie

Breakfast No. 1
½ medium apple
2 slices toast, white
2 tsp. orange marmalade
Coffee or tea

Breakfast No. 2
Same as 800-Calorie Diet

Lunch No. 1
½ cup soup, pepperpot
Lobster salad (3 oz.)
12 tiny cheese crackers
Coffee or tea

Lunch No. 2
Same as 800-Calorie Diet

Dinner No. 1
½ cup soup, pepperpot
1 slice ham, baked
Gruyere cheese (1 oz.)
2 saltines
Coffee or tea

Dinner No. 2
Any No. 2 meal on the 600-Calorie Diet

1200 Calorie

Breakfast No. 1
½ med. honeydew melon
2 eggs (poached, soft or hard)
Coffee or tea

Breakfast No. 2
Same as 800-Calorie Diet

Lunch No. 1
½ cup soup, lentil
1 cup Yogurt, strawberry
1 sugar wafer cookie
Coffee or tea

Lunch No. 2
Same as 800-Calorie Diet

Dinner No. 1
½ med. honeydew melon
½ cup soup, lentil
1 med. lean veal chop, braised
1 cup spinach, cooked
Coffee or tea

Dinner No. 2
Any No. 2 meal on the 600-Calorie Diet

MIRACLE DIET MENUS

DAY TWENTY-FOUR

600 Calorie

Breakfast No. 1
2 slices bacon, broiled
Coffee or tea

Breakfast No. 2
V-8 juice (4 oz.)

Lunch No. 1
Pork liver, broiled (3/8" thick)
Coffee or tea

Lunch No. 2
1 cup consommé

Dinner No. 1
Pork liver, broiled (3/8" slice)
Coffee or tea

Dinner No. 2
3 oz. farmer cheese

800 Calorie

Breakfast No. 1
½ grapefruit, small
1 tsp. sugar
½ English muffin or bagel
¼ tsp. butter
½ cup skim milk
Coffee or tea

Breakfast No. 2
2 canned pear halves

Lunch No. 1
½ grapefruit, small with sprinkle of cinnamon
½ med. egg, hard-cooked
1 med. tomato sliced with 2 tbs. wine vinegar
½ med. potato, baked
1 tsp. butter
Coffee or tea

Lunch No. 2
¼ cantaloupe
1 slice toast, light rye or whole wheat
½ tsp. grape jelly

Dinner No. 1
Lean roast beef (4 oz.)
½ medium potato, baked
Coffee or tea

Dinner No. 2
Any No. 2 meal on the 600-Calorie Diet

1000 Calorie

Breakfast No. 1
1 cup fresh strawberries
1 tsp. sugar
1 slice toast, light rye or whole wheat
1 tsp. orange marmalade
2/3 cup skim milk
Coffee or tea

Breakfast No. 2
Same as 800-Calorie Diet

Lunch No. 1
½ cup soup, pepperpot
Fillet of sole, broiled (8 oz.)
Coffee or tea

Lunch No. 2
Same as 800-Calorie Diet

Dinner No. 1
¼ cantaloupe
2/3 cup soup, barley
1 tongue sandwich (2 slices rye bread)
Watercress & 1 tbs. mustard
Coffee or tea

Dinner No. 2
Any No. 2 meal on the 600-Calorie Diet

1200 Calorie

Breakfast No. 1
½ honeydew melon
2 slices smoked salmon
½ cup skim milk
1 saltine cracker
Coffee or tea

Breakfast No. 2
Same as 800-Calorie Diet

Lunch No. 1
1 cup Yogurt, strawberry
1 medium egg (hard-boiled)
Coffee or tea

Lunch No. 2
Same as 800-Calorie Diet

Dinner No. 1
2 lean pork chops, small, broiled
½ cup brown rice, cooked
½ cup fresh peas, cooked
1 medium nectarine
Coffee or tea

Dinner No. 2
Any No. 2 meal on the 600-Calorie Diet

MIRACLE DIET MENUS

DAY TWENTY-FIVE

600 Calorie

Breakfast No. 1
Onion omelet (1 egg)
Coffee or tea

Breakfast No. 2
Beef broth (4 oz.)

Lunch No. 1
2 pieces luncheon meat (3/16" each)
Coffee or tea

Lunch No. 2
¼ cup cottage cheese with vegetables

Dinner No. 1
Beef kidney (2 oz.)
Coffee or tea

Dinner No. 2
Blueberry muffin

800 Calorie

Breakfast No. 1
4 prunes, stewed (without sugar)
1 slice toast, light rye or whole wheat
½ tsp. grape jelly
Coffee or tea

Breakfast No. 2
½ cup cole slaw
3 rye or wheat thins

Lunch No. 1
½ cup tomato juice
Crabmeat, canned or fresh (4 oz.)
lemon wedge
½ cup wax beans, cooked
4 rye or wheat thins
Coffee or tea

Lunch No. 2
½ cup orange juice, frozen, diluted
3 wheat or rye thins

Dinner No. 1
Chicken livers, broiled (4 oz.)
1 cup zucchini, cooked
Coffee or tea

Dinner No. 2
Any No. 2 meal on the 600-Calorie Diet

1000 Calorie

Breakfast No. 1
½ honeydew melon, med. size
1 slice Zweibach
½ cup skim milk
Coffee or tea

Breakfast No. 2
Same as 800-Calorie Diet

Lunch No. 1
1 cup Manhattan clam chowder
6 med. fresh shrimp, boiled
1 tsp. lemon juice
1 medium egg, hard
2 rye or wheat thins
Coffee or tea

Lunch No. 2
Same as 800-Calorie Diet

Dinner No. 1
¼ cup tomato juice
Chicken, broiled (6 oz.)
½ cup fresh peas, cooked
Coffee or tea

Dinner No. 2
Any No. 2 meal on the 600-Calorie Diet

1200 Calorie

Breakfast No. 1
½ honeydew melon
1 slice baked ham
½ cup skim milk
Coffee or tea

Breakfast No. 2
Same as 800-Calorie Diet

Lunch No. 1
¼ cantaloupe
1 cup Yogurt, coffee or vanilla
1 slice baked ham   *or*   corned beef
Coffee or tea

Lunch No. 2
Same as 800-Calorie Diet

Dinner No. 1
1 cup consommé
Halibut steak, broiled (5 oz.)
1 medium ear of corn
½ cup skim milk
Coffee or tea

Dinner No. 2
Any No. 2 meal on the 600-Calorie Diet

MIRACLE DIET MENUS

DAY TWENTY-SIX

600 Calorie	800 Calorie	1000 Calorie	1200 Calorie
Breakfast No. 1	*Breakfast No. 1*	*Breakfast No. 1*	*Breakfast No. 1*
All-wheat cereal (4 oz.)	½ cup fresh cherries	½ grapefruit, small	½ honeydew melon
Skim milk (4 oz.)	1 medium egg	2 tsp. sugar	1 slice American cheese
Coffee or tea	1 piece Zweibach toast	1 tsp. cream cheese	1 slice smoked salmon
	¼ tsp. jelly	1 slice toast, rye or whole wheat	Coffee or tea
	Coffee or tea	½ cup skim milk	
		Coffee or tea	
Breakfast No. 2	*Breakfast No. 2*	*Breakfast No. 2*	*Breakfast No. 2*
Tomato cocktail (4 oz.)	1 cup consommé	Same as 800-Calorie Diet	Same as 800-Calorie Diet
	2 slices Zweibach toast		
Lunch No. 1	*Lunch No. 1*	*Lunch No. 1*	*Lunch No. 1*
1 slice American cheese	2/3 cup fresh strawberries	Veal cutlet, broiled (4 oz.)	½ honeydew melon
Coffee or tea	2 tsp. sour cream	1 large celery stalk	1 cup Yogurt, coffee or vanilla
	½ cup soup, pepperpot or chicken-rice	Coffee or tea	2 rye or wheat thins
	2 slices smoked salmon		Coffee or tea
	lemon wedge		
	Coffee or tea		
Lunch No. 2	*Lunch No. 2*	*Lunch No. 2*	*Lunch No. 2*
1 cup soup, julienne	1 cup consommé	Same as 800-Calorie Diet	Same as 800-Calorie Diet
	1 medium apple		
Dinner No. 1	*Dinner No. 1*	*Dinner No. 1*	*Dinner No. 1*
Heart, beef (1 oz.) (2" long)	Fillet of sole, broiled (4 oz.) *or*	¼ cup soup, chicken vegetable	1 medium tangerine
Coffee or tea	1 slice baked ham *or*	1 med. veal chop (lean), braised	Halibut steak (5 oz.) broiled
	1 slice corned beef	½ cup white rice, cooked	½ cup brown rice, cooked
	½ cup succotash, canned	Coffee or tea	1 cup green beans, cooked
	1 cup green beans, cooked		1 large celery stalk
	Coffee or tea		Coffee or tea
Dinner No. 2	*Dinner No. 2*	*Dinner No. 2*	*Dinner No. 2*
1 cup beef broth, hot or cold	Any No. 2 meal on the 600-Calorie Diet	Any No. 2 meal on the 600-Calorie Diet	Any No. 2 meal on the 600-Calorie Diet

110

MIRACLE DIET MENUS

DAY TWENTY-SEVEN

600 Calorie

Breakfast No. 1
1 slice toast, wheat
lightly buttered
Coffee or tea

Breakfast No. 2
Chicken broth (4 oz.)

Lunch No. 1
Fruit plate on lettuce (sliced
peach, pear)
Coffee or tea

Lunch No. 2
2 slices Canadian bacon

Dinner No. 1
Eel, smoked (2 oz.)
Coffee or tea

Dinner No. 2
English muffin, ½
with 1 tsp. diet jelly

800 Calorie

Breakfast No. 1
½ cup loganberries, canned or
fresh
1 tsp. sugar
2/3 cup skim milk
3 rye or wheat thins
Coffee or tea

Breakfast No. 2
3 rye or wheat thins
4 tsp. blu-cheese spread

Lunch No. 1
1 medium fresh plum
1 cup consommé   or
   2 large celery stalks   or
   4 radishes
Calf's liver, broiled (3 oz.)   or
4 rye or wheat thins   or
   2 rye crisp (double squares)
Coffee or tea

Lunch No. 2
2 peach halves, canned
4 wheat thins or rye thins

Dinner No. 1
Lean pot roast (5 oz.)
1 large celery stalk
Coffee or tea

Dinner No. 2
Any No. 2 meal on the 600-
Calorie Diet

1000 Calorie

Breakfast No. 1
2 eggs (soft, poached or hard)
2 rye crisp (double squares)
Coffee or tea

Breakfast No. 2
Same as 800-Calorie Diet

Lunch No. 1
Broiled beef (4 oz.)
1 large celery stalk
Coffee or tea

Lunch No. 2
Same as 800-Calorie Diet

Dinner No. 1
1 cup Manhattan clam chowder
Kippered herring (3 oz.)
5 artichoke hearts, canned
2 celery stalks, large
Coffee or tea

Dinner No. 2
Any No. 2 meal on the 600-
Calorie Diet

1200 Calorie

Breakfast No. 1
½ honeydew melon
½ cup Yogurt, plain or coffee
1 slice toast, rye or whole wheat
Coffee or tea

Breakfast No. 2
Same as 800-Calorie Diet

Lunch No. 1
1/3 cup creamed cottage cheese
1 large romaine leaf
6 asparagus spears
2 slices smoked salmon
½ cup fruit gelatin
1 large gingersnap cookie
Coffee or tea

Lunch No. 2
Same as 800-Calorie Diet

Dinner No. 1
½ cup Yogurt, strawberry
2 soft shell crabs, fried
6 asparagus spears
Coffee or tea

Dinner No. 2
Any No. 2 meal on the 600-
Calorie Diet

MIRACLE DIET MENUS

DAY TWENTY-EIGHT

600 Calorie

Breakfast No. 1

1 slice ham
Coffee or tea

Breakfast No. 2

Loganberry juice (4 oz.)

Lunch No. 1

1 frankfurter, boiled or broiled
Coffee or tea

Lunch No. 2

1 cup bouillon
4 soda type crackers

Dinner No. 1

10 pieces meat balls
  (miniature)
Coffee or tea

Dinner No. 2

Cheese wafers

---

800 Calorie

Breakfast No. 1

½ medium apple
1 medium egg
4 rye or wheat thins
Coffee or tea

Breakfast No. 2

1 gingersnap cookie, large
2/3 cup skim milk

Lunch No. 1

1 slice baked ham   *or*
  1 slice corned beef
½ med. potato, baked with
  grated Parmesan cheese
1 carrot, strips
1/3 cup skim milk
Coffee or tea

Lunch No. 2

1 cup consommé
5 cucumber slices
1 celery stalk
1 medium fresh plum
3 rye or wheat thins

Dinner No. 1

3 slices bacon, broiled
1 cup zucchini, cooked
6 asparagus spears
Coffee or tea

Dinner No. 2

Any No. 2 meal on the 600-
  Calorie Diet

1000 Calorie

Breakfast No. 1

¼ cantaloupe
1 medium egg (poached, soft-
  cooked or hard)
1 med. slice baked ham
Coffee or tea

Breakfast No. 2

Same as 800-Calorie Diet

Lunch No. 1

Leg of veal, roasted,
  3 medium slices
2/3 cup brussels sprouts, cooked
Coffee or tea

Lunch No. 2

Same as 800-Calorie Diet

Dinner No. 1

1 salmon steak, baked
1 medium ear corn
2 large celery stalks
Coffee or tea

Dinner No. 2

Any No. 2 meal on the 600-
  Calorie Diet

1200 Calorie

Breakfast No. 1

1 cup fresh pineapple, diced
1 slice American cheese
2 saltine crackers
½ cup skim milk
Coffee or tea

Breakfast No. 2

Same as 800-Calorie Diet

Lunch No. 1

Kippered herring, (3 oz.)
1/3 cup creamed cottage cheese
1 large romaine leaf
2 sugar wafer cookies
Coffee or tea

Lunch No. 2

Same as 800-Calorie Diet

Dinner No. 1

1 frankfurter
½ cup scalloped potatoes
1 medium tomato
¾ cup sour cherries, canned
Coffee or tea

Dinner No. 2

Any No. 2 meal on the 600-
  Calorie Diet

MIRACLE DIET MENUS

DAY TWENTY-NINE

600 Calorie	800 Calorie	1000 Calorie	1200 Calorie
Breakfast No. 1	*Breakfast No. 1*	*Breakfast No. 1*	*Breakfast No. 1*
1 slice rye toast lightly buttered Coffee or tea	¼ cantaloupe ½ cup Wheaties 1 tsp. sugar 2/3 cup skim milk Coffee or tea	2 peach halves, canned 1 slice French toast 1 tsp. orange marmalade *or* 1 tsp. strawberry jam Coffee or tea	½ medium apple 1 slice bacon, broiled Chicken livers, broiled (4 oz.) Coffee or tea
Breakfast No. 2	*Breakfast No. 2*	*Breakfast No. 2*	*Breakfast No. 2*
Carrot juice (4 oz.)	1 sugar wafer cookie 2/3 cup skim milk	Same as 800-Calorie Diet	Same as 800-Calorie Diet
Lunch No. 1	*Lunch No. 1*	*Lunch No. 1*	*Lunch No. 1*
1 head cheese (1/16" thick) Coffee or tea	½ cup Yogurt, strawberry 3 tbs. corned beef hash 3 rye or wheat thins Coffee or tea	1 cup soup, onion ½ ave. chicken breast, roasted ½ cup fruit flavored gelatin Coffee or tea	1 cup consommé Gruyere cheese (1 oz.) 2 slices melba toast ½ medium apple ½ cup banana whip pudding Coffee or tea
Lunch No. 2	*Lunch No. 2*	*Lunch No. 2*	*Lunch No. 2*

1 slice beef liver, broiled
  (3/8" thick)
	¼ cup tomato juice
	1 cup diced cantaloupe *or*
	  1 medium fresh plum
	2 sugar wafer cookies
		Same as 800-Calorie Diet	Same as 800-Calorie Diet

Dinner No. 1	*Dinner No. 1*	*Dinner No. 1*	*Dinner No. 1*
Pate with herbs (1 oz.) (Le Parfait) Coffee or tea	Salmon steak, broiled (4 oz.) 1 cup turnip greens, cooked Coffee or tea	Smoked white fish (3 oz.) ¾ cup mashed potatoes (with milk) 1 cup broccoli, cooked 4 radishes Coffee or tea	½ cup soup, pepperpot Bass, baked (5 oz.) 1 cup zucchini, cooked 1 large celery stalk ½ pear, canned Coffee or tea
Dinner No. 2	*Dinner No. 2*	*Dinner No. 2*	*Dinner No. 2*
Skim milk (8 oz.)	Any No. 2 meal on the 600-Calorie Diet	Any No. 2 meal on the 600-Calorie Diet	Any No. 2 meal on the 600-Calorie Diet

MIRACLE DIET MENUS

DAY THIRTY

	600 Calorie	800 Calorie	1000 Calorie	1200 Calorie
Breakfast No. 1	1 egg, fried (greaseless) Coffee or tea	1/3 cup fresh grapefruit sections 1 tsp. sugar ½ medium bran *or* corn muffin ½ tsp. grape jelly ½ cup skim milk Coffee or tea	2 pear halves, canned ½ medium egg (soft-cooked or hard) 1 slice toast, white 1 tsp. strawberry jam *or* orange marmalade Coffee or tea	½ honeydew melon 1 bagel 1 tsp. grape jelly Coffee or tea
Breakfast No. 2	Vegetable juice (4 oz.)	¼ cantaloupe 1 cup consommé ½ slice Swiss cheese	Same as 800-Calorie Diet	Same as 800-Calorie Diet
Lunch No. 1	Stuffed tomato with 2 oz. cottage cheese Coffee or tea	1 cup Yogurt, plain 1 slice smoked salmon with lemon wedge 2 sugar wafer cookies Coffee or tea	1 cup Manhattan clam chowder ½ cup creamed cottage cheese ½ medium cucumber 2 rye or wheat thins Coffee or tea	2-egg cheese omelet 1 rye or wheat thin Coffee or tea
Lunch No. 2	1 slice calf's liver (3/8" thick)	1 cup diced cantaloupe *or* 1 medium fresh plum ½ cup soup, clear chicken 1 rye crisp (double square) 1 celery stalk	Same as 800-Calorie Diet	Same as 800-Calorie Diet
Dinner No. 1	10 pieces Gefilte fish (miniatures) Coffee or tea	1 cup consommé 1 med. lean veal chop, braised ½ cup mushrooms Coffee or tea	½ cup soup, all vegetable Crabmeat, fresh or canned (8 oz.) 6 asparagus spears Coffee or tea	1 cup tomato juice Bass, baked (5 oz.) ½ cup brown rice, cooked 2 large celery stalks Coffee or tea
Dinner No. 2	Orange muffin	Any No. 2 meal on the 600-Calorie Diet	Any No. 2 meal on the 600-Calorie Diet	Any No. 2 meal on the 600-Calorie Diet

114

Miracle Step Four

Starting with the 1200-calorie Miracle Diet, select those days that appeal to your taste and renumber them for your use. Make a shopping list for the first week. Feel free to substitute corresponding meals from other days. Do the same, if you wish, with corresponding dishes in the same meal. Go through this same procedure if you shift down to any of the calorie levels. Make a chart so that you can follow your weight loss progress from day to day. If one week's loss drops below par (1 percent of weight), make the shift.

How to Cook What You Like, the Way You Like It— and Lose Weight

Are you limited to the thirty days of menus listed on the previous pages?

The answer is *no*.

There is no limit to the types of food you can eat on the Miracle Diet. There are other limits:

1. You must eat six meals a day.
2. You must stay within the calorie limits set.
3. You must select foods with the greatest nutritional content per calorie.

With these limits in mind, you can create any number of delicious meals.

The Calorie Limits

Each of the six meals on each of the four Miracle Diets has been organized under strict calorie limitations. Here they are:

	600-CALORIE DIET	800-CALORIE DIET	1000-CALORIE DIET	1200-CALORIE DIET
BREAKFAST #1	100	150	200	250
BREAKFAST #2	65	90	90	90
LUNCH #1	75	200	250	300
LUNCH #2	90	90	90	90
DINNER #1	200	200	300	400
DINNER #2	70	70	70	70

These calorie limits must be observed when making substitutions. Obviously, there is not leeway for elaborate culinary creations on the #2 meals. But Breakfast #1, Lunch #1, and Dinner #1 are wide open in that a modest portion of almost any nutritional dish will fit within the calorie specifications.

Now, I'm not talking about starchy entrees. The spaghettis and macaronis are out. So are the meat pies and any other heavy-with-flour dishes. The reason is that you are not only very likely exceeding calorie limits, but you are using up calorie allowances on foods that are low man on the totem pole when measured in nutritional value.

A Trustworthy Nutritional Barometer

Fats and carbohydrates are necessary foods, but the body's number one priority is protein. Fats and carbohydrates can produce energy, but they cannot build body cells. Only protein can build body cells. Protein can also be converted into energy.

So you cannot go wrong with protein if you are measuring for nutritional value. We are not all expert nutritionists. There is no such thing as a nutritional thermometer that you can jab into food and take a reading. We have to use some rules of thumb.

Later we will discuss some specific foods that give a tremendous amount of nutritional mileage per calorie. Meanwhile there are three rules of thumb that are helpful:

1. Proteins should be favored over fats and carbohydrates.
2. Some fruit and vegetable should be included daily.
3. Food should be as fresh and as local as is feasible or possible.

The Miracle Protein Diet

Following these rules of thumb, it would appear that a six-meal Miracle Diet consisting almost entirely of protein would be quite effective.

It certainly is.

The most dramatic successes my clients have enjoyed have been on diets where 70 to 80 percent of the calorie quota is in protein.

I am now going to give you a list of these high protein foods together with their calories per portion and a peek into their protein-fat-carbohydrate composition.

With this list you can create your own menus for a Miracle Protein Diet. All you need to do is to stay within the above calorie limits per meal.

(REMEMBER that you must start on the 1200-calorie Miracle Diet and shift down only when your weight loss is less than it should be as explained in the previous chapter.)

I promise you: THIS IS THE FASTEST AND EASIEST DIET YOU CAN GO ON. However, there are some people with medical problems—usually kidney related, such as the gout—who may not be able to tolerate a high protein diet. If in doubt, consult your physician. One good precaution is to drink plenty of water during and between meals.

THE MIRACLE PROTEIN DIET

FOOD	PORTION	CALORIES	PROTEIN	FAT	CARBO-HYDRATES
			(Composition in grams)		
DAIRY					
Milk, skimmed	one cup	90	9	0	13
Buttermilk	one cup	90	9	0	13
Cottage Cheese	one cup (un-creamed)	195	38	1	6
Eggs (whole)	1	75	7	5	0
Egg whites	1	15	4	0	0
Egg yolk	1	60	3	5	0
MEAT					
Veal cutlet, broiled	3 oz.	185	23	9	0

Food	Portion	Calories	Protein	Fat	Carbo-hydrates
					(Composition in grams)
MEAT *(cont.)*					
Chicken, broiled	3½ oz.	135	24	4	0
Beef liver, fried	2 slices (2 × 2¼ × ⅜ inches)	170	20	8	4
Beef, canned corned	3 slices (3 × 2 × ¼ inches)	185	22	10	0
Hamburger— lean ground	4 oz.	185	23	10	0
Round steak, broiled	1 slice (4½ × 3½ × ½ inches)	260	29	15	0
Lamb chop, lean, broiled	2½ oz.	125	19	5	0
Leg of lamb, lean	3 oz.	160	24	6	0
Turkey	3½ oz.	175	33	4	0
SOUP					
Broth or con-sommé	¾ cup (coffee cup)	20	4	0	2
FISH					
Scallops, boiled or broiled	3½ oz.	80	16	0	3
Cod steak, broiled with butter	4 oz. (before cooking)	170	29	5	0
Swordfish, broiled with butter	3½ oz.	175	28	6	0
Tuna, water packed	⅝ cup	125	28	1	0
Lobster	⅔ cup	95	19	2	0
Shrimp	3 oz.	100	21	1	1
Oysters, stew	15 oysters	160	20	4	8
Crabmeat	3 oz.	85	15	2	1
Clams	3 oz.	65	11	1	2
Bluefish	3 oz.	135	24	4	0

All the Vegetables You Can Eat

If you go on this Miracle Protein Diet, I will give you an unexpected bonus:

You can eat all you want of the following vegetables:

Asparagus	Turnip Greens
Cucumbers	Spinach
Celery	Radishes
Endive	Romaine
Fennel	Parsley
Watercress	Tomatoes
	Lettuce

These vegetables are high in vitamins and minerals, low in calories. They are so low in calories, in fact, they demand almost as many calories to be digested as they supply.

So I am not being overly generous when I say—go to it. There is little likelihood that even a real "wolfer" can break the calorie limit significantly with extra portions of these healthful vegetables.

Of course, you are not limited to only these vegetables. From 5 percent to 10 percent of your total calorie limit can be devoted to fruits, fruit juices and vegetables without detracting from the weight-melting power of the Miracle Protein Diet.

Other vegetables that are on my preferred list and modest portion of which can be enjoyed twice a day are:

Cabbage	Summer squash
Bamboo shoots	Bean sprouts
Broccoli	Cauliflower
Chard	Snow peas
String beans	Italian green beans

The modest portion is equal to about 50 calories on the average for these vegetables. Most are available in frozen food departments of supermarkets. Of course, they should be bought fresh wherever and whenever available.

Utilize the same fruits and fruit juices as listed in the 30-day menus.

Mrs. P. writes:

My husband and I have been on The Miracle Protein Diet for two weeks. We have lost 18 pounds between us. We'll stay on 1200 calories at this rate. He says it's a man's diet with all the steak, lamb and veal. Neither of us have been as hungry on six diet meals as we used to be on three squares a day.

The Mystery of Fresh Foods

I always feel a little uneasy about insisting on fresh foods wherever possible. Certainly there are millions of healthy people who live on canned, frozen and nearly fresh foods.

Nobody has ever proved that foods indigenous to an area are any more valuable than those freighted in from across a continent. But I'll still stick to my guns.

An interesting study was recently completed in Guam and American Samoa. A special Pacific Islands task force recommended to the December, 1969, White House Conference on Food, Nutrition and Health that grants be made available to establish farming with low interest loans. The goal is to preserve indigenous food products in these islands.

It seems that everything was fine when these people lived mainly on the food that grew naturally in their islands. They had few, if any, nutritional problems.

However, with commercial development, importation of food, and European and American influences, nutritional problems developed.

It was personally gratifying to me to see that the task force recommended a return to indigenous foods rather than an acceleration of imports. I feel more comfortable now when I tell a client, "Check your fresh fruit and vegetable counters before you buy canned or frozen—and look for the word 'local.' "

Your Favorite Recipe May Have a Place on the Miracle Diet

If you eat six meals a day; if you stay within the calorie limits; if you eat nutritional foods; then you are on the Miracle Diet.

Nothing says you cannot enjoy Shrimp Supreme, or Roast Long Island Duckling, or Chicken Breasts Amandine.

A recipe particularly rich in fats and carbohydrates will definitely require you to go easy in the size of the portion.

Beef dishes are higher in calories than veal, lamb or poultry dishes, so they, too, require a cautious serving.

You can evaluate your own recipes for appropriateness for the Miracle Diet and as to whether small or modest portions are indicated by examining the ingredients.

"Go" ingredients are salt, pepper, other spices and herbs. Fine, too, are onion, celery, lemon, vanilla, other flavor extracts, garlic, green pepper, tomato or tomato paste, pimento, chives, parsley, etc.

"Stop" ingredients are flour, sugar, bread crumbs and other starches or sweeteners.

I want to go on record as encouraging you to prepare your favorite recipes. Your enjoyment of the food you eat while on the Miracle Diet is important to your success. I leave it to your good judgment to eliminate the "stop" recipes that are too starchy or sweet. And I leave it to your good judgment to hold your portion down to a modest four ounces or less.

Otherwise, let your imagination go hand-in-hand with your taste pleasures.

Here Are Nearly 100 Exciting Recipes

To give you an example of what you can eat on the Miracle Diet I have borrowed from the files of wife, friends and relatives and screened their favorite recipes for nutritional and taste value. If, in the process, I have divulged any family secrets or inadvertently plagiarized from private sources, all I can say is—think of all the people who will now be benefiting.

The appetizers and soups can be used for Lunch No. 2. The entrees are suitable in some cases for Lunch No. 1 and in others, Dinners No. 1. The salads are suitable for Lunch No. 1 or Lunch No. 2. The desserts are suitable for Dinner No. 2.

In all cases take less than a proportionate serving. That is, if a recipe serves four to six, take less than one sixth of the dish for yourself. If it serves four, as most do, take one fifth or one sixth for yourself. Avoid seconds. Take your seconds, if you must, the next day.

Ready? Begin.

APPETIZERS

Shrimp Supreme

1 lb. raw shrimp	⅛ tsp. pepper
3 tbs. olive oil	½ tsp. salt
2 tbs. melted butter	½ tsp. monosodium glutamate
2 tbs. lemon juice	2 tbs. chopped parsley
1 clove garlic, minced	

Remove shell and clean shrimp. Wash and drain. Mix all other ingredients in a shallow pan. Marinate shrimp in this mixture for several hours, stirring frequently. Broil in marinade just until shrimp turn pink. Serve on toothpicks. Serves 6.

Pungent Cucumbers

2 medium-size cucumbers	½ tsp. salt
4 tbs. cider vinegar	¼ tsp. pepper
1 tbs. sugar	

Peel cucumber and cut into very thin slices. Mix other ingredients in a bowl. Add cucumber slices and stir. Pour off vinegar mixture and arrange neatly on serving plates. Serves 4–6.

Celestial Stuffed Raw Mushrooms

12 medium-size mushrooms	⅛ tsp. curry powder
2 tbs. Camembert cheese	⅛ tsp. nutmeg
1 tbs. Roquefort cheese	2 tbs. chopped walnuts
2 tbs. chopped celery	parsley
½ tsp. Worcestershire sauce	

Wash mushrooms; do not peel if very fresh. Remove stems and reserve for future use. Dry mushrooms well with paper toweling. Cream cheeses together and add spices and celery. Fill mushroom caps with cheese mixture. Sprinkle nuts on top mixture, pressing down gently. Arrange on small plates with sprigs of parsley as garnish. Serve cold. Serves 6.

Cucumber Yogurt Appetizer

2 medium-size cucumbers
2 young green onions
1/4 tsp. chili powder
1/4 tsp. cumin powder

1/4 tsp. powdered cloves
1 c. yogurt
salt and pepper to taste

Peel cucumber and cut into thin slices. Arrange attractively on serving plates. Cover cucumbers with several paper towels, weighted down by a rather heavy plate. Chop green onions fine and add to yogurt with other ingredients. Stir well. Remove plate and paper towels from cucumber slices and top with yogurt sauce. Serve cold.

Fluffy Cheese Dip

1/2 lb. cream cheese
1/4 lb. Roquefort cheese
1/2 lb. pimento cheese

2 tbs. butter
2 tbs. honey
1/2 tsp. Worcestershire sauce

Melt cheese in upper part of double boiler, stirring constantly. Add butter, honey, and Worcestershire sauce and beat until fluffy. Serve as a dip with low calorie crackers or pieces of raw vegetables.

Cantaloupe and Prosciutto

1 sm. cantaloupe

1/4 lb. prosciutto, sliced thin

Cut chilled melon into 8 small wedges and remove seeds. Serve with prosciutto. Serves 4.

Tomato Cocktail Excellente

1 pt. plain tomato juice
1/8 tsp. salt
1/4 tsp. sugar
1 lemon

1/2 tsp. each chopped basil, thyme, marjoram, summer savory and monosodium glutamate
1 tsp. chopped chives

Add herbs, salt and sugar to tomato juice and allow to steep at room temperature for one hour, stirring occasionally. Add juice of lemon and refrigerate for several hours. Strain before serving. Serves 4.

Avocado Versatile

½ avocado pear
1 sm. tomato
1 tsp. onion
1 tsp. chopped basil

1 tsp. monosodium glutamate
1 tsp. lemon juice
1 tsp. olive oil
Pinch of salt

Peel and mash avocado well. Add remaining ingredients and chill. May be served as a dip, or spread on crackers or bread rounds.

Yogurt and Herb Dip

2 cups yogurt
1 tsp. caraway seeds
2 tsp. minced onion

2 tsp. minced chives
¼ tsp. chopped or dried thyme
salt to taste

Blend all ingredients together and chill for several hours. Serve with a variety of raw vegetables.

SOUPS

Hearty Garlic Soup

1 c. beef consommé
½ c. water
1 clove garlic

2 eggs
2 thin slices of tomato
Paprika

Heat consommé and water in saucepan. Crush garlic into soup and bring to a boil. Turn heat down so that liquid is just barely bubbling. Break eggs gently into liquid being careful not to break yolk. Spoon liquid over egg until it is cooked (about three minutes). Remove eggs with slotted spoon and place in soup plates. Strain soup over egg. Float tomato slice on top of soup. Sprinkle with paprika. Serves 2.

Italian Clam Soup

1 c. condensed tomato soup	½ clove garlic
1 c. minced clams	½ tsp. chopped parsley
1 sm. bottle clam juice	1 tbs. grated Parmesan cheese

Heat tomato soup and clam juice in a saucepan. Crush garlic into soup and bring to a boil. Reduce heat to simmer and add clams and their juice. Simmer for one minute. Pour soup into soup plates. Sprinkle with parsley and cheese. Serves 4.

Summer Salad Soup

1 clove garlic	½ c. thinly sliced celery
3 tomatoes, finely chopped	2 tbs. olive oil
½ unpeeled cucumber, thinly sliced	2 tbs. white vinegar
	Salt and pepper
1 tbs. chives	2 c. tomato juice

Rub large bowl with garlic; stick toothpick through garlic and leave in bowl. Add all other ingredients in order and mix well. Chill 3 hours. Remove garlic before serving.

Spinach Soup

1 pkg. frozen chopped spinach	1 envelope chicken broth mix
½ lb. lean ground beef	1 c. water
2 tsp. soy sauce	1 egg

Defrost and then drain frozen spinach. Brown meat with soy sauce. Add broth mix, water, and drained spinach. Boil gently for two more minutes, adding a little more water if necessary. Beat egg in a cup. Remove soup from heat and beat in egg. Heat soup for ten seconds but do not let it boil. Serves 4.

Chinese Egg Drop Soup

2 chicken bouillon cubes or packets	1 beaten egg
	2 cups boiling water

Dissolve bouillon in boiling water in saucepan. Drop beaten egg from a fork about 5 inches above saucepan. Reduce heat and simmer for five minutes.

Icy Vegetable Soup

3 tbs. salad or olive oil
1 c. cold canned bouillon
3 c. tomato juice
1 sm. onion, minced
1 c. celery stalk chopped fine

1 large green pepper, chopped fine
2 tbs. lemon juice
Salt, pepper, to taste
1 tomato, cut up
1 cucumber, diced

Combine all ingredients, taste for seasoning and chill for at least 3 hours. To serve, turn into a glass bowl or chilled tureen, and garnish with a few ice cubes. Serves 6.

Hamburg Soup

1 lb. lean chopped meat
1 chopped onion
1 green pepper, chopped
1 stalk celery, chopped
2 c. boiling water

1 pkg. frozen mixed vegetables
1 bay leaf
2 cups fresh tomatoes, cut up or
    tomato juice
Salt and pepper to taste

Brown chopped meat, breaking up with a fork. Add onion, celery, and green pepper and brown a little. Add boiling water and then remaining ingredients. Simmer for 30 minutes. Remove bay leaf. Soup may be thickened with a tablespoon of flour mixed with a little milk, if desired.

Shrimp Consommé

2 envelopes chicken broth mix
2 cups boiling water
6 large cooked shrimp

½ pkg. frozen peas
4 thin slices lemon

Add broth mix and peas to boiling water in saucepan. Continue to let boil gently, until peas are cooked. Dice shrimp and add to soup. Cook only about another minute or so, just to heat shrimp. Pour into serving cups, floating thin slice of lemon on top. Serves 4.

Creamy Venetian Soup

2 c. undiluted beef consommé
2 egg yolks
3 tbs. heavy cream

½ tsp. concentrated beef extract
3 tbs. grated Parmesan cheese

Have water boiling in bottom of double boiler. Pour consommé into top of double boiler. Beat egg yolk, cream, and beef extract in cup and add to consommé. Stir well. Bring almost to boiling point, but do not allow to boil. Sprinkle with Parmesan cheese and serve immediately. Serves 4.

Salmon Bisque

2 slices bacon
2 carrots, diced
2 onions, chopped fine
2 stalks celery with leaves, diced
2 c. fresh or canned tomatoes
1 green pepper, cut fine

1 pimento, cut fine
1 minced clove garlic
1 qt. stock or vegetable cooking water
1 c. salmon, flaked and boned

Cut bacon into bits and fry (pan-broil in utensil large enough to hold soup). Sauté all vegetables and seasonings with bacon (except tomatoes). Add stock or vegetable cooking water and tomatoes and continue to simmer gently until vegetables are tender. Immediately before serving add canned salmon. Serves 6.

ENTREES

Tomatoed Scrambled Eggs

3 medium size tomatoes
1 clove garlic, minced
2 tbs. olive oil

1 tsp. brown sugar
Salt and pepper to taste
6 eggs

Peel the tomatoes and cut into small pieces. Add the garlic to olive oil in frying pan and sauté until yellow. Add the tomatoes and seasonings, simmering until the tomatoes are soft. Beat the eggs and stir into the tomatoes, to cook until the mixture is set. Serves 4.

Veal Chops Supreme

8 sm. veal chops	1 tbs. olive oil
Salt and pepper	1 clove garlic, crushed
1 tsp. paprika	2 tbs. chopped parsley
1 tbs. butter	1 c. white wine

Season chops with salt, pepper and paprika and brown in butter and olive oil in frying pan until golden brown. Drain on paper towel. Line shallow casserole with aluminum foil. Arrange chops in casserole, placing crushed garlic and parsley on each chop. Add wine and cover pan. Bake in 350° oven for 45 minutes. Serve with grilled tomato slices. Serves 4.

Chicken Breasts Amandine

4 whole chicken breasts	¼ tsp. rosemary
Juice of 1 lemon	1 tbs. chopped parsley
Salt and pepper	1 tsp. paprika
1 clove garlic	4 tbs. melted butter
½ tsp. poultry seasoning	½ c. sliced almonds
½ tsp. thyme	

Rub chicken with lemon juice. Sprinkle with salt and pepper. Rub with cut clove of garlic. Sprinkle with remainder of seasonings. Let stand 2 hours. Preheat broiler; place broiler pan as far from heat as possible. Place chicken on broiler pan and brush with melted butter. Broil slowly about 20 minutes on each side. 10 minutes before serving sprinkle with almonds. Baste with additional butter during broiling time, if desired. Serves 4.

Honey-Mint Lamb Chops

4 loin lamb chops, cut 1 inch thick	1 tbs. vinegar
½ c. water	¾ c. honey
	¼ c. chopped mint

Heat water and vinegar; add honey, stirring well, and then add chopped mint. Cook slowly for five minutes. Place chops on broiling pan about three inches from heat, and broil for about 15 minutes. Baste frequently with sauce while broiling. Serves 4.

Florentine Broiled Fillets

2 pkg. frozen chopped spinach
1 sm. minced onion
4 tbs. melted butter
1½ lbs. haddock fillets

2 tsp. lemon juice
1½ c. grated American cheese
½ c. milk

Cook spinach as directed on package. Drain. Sauté onion in 2 tbs. of the butter until soft; add to spinach. Preheat broiler. Place fish fillets in a greased shallow baking pan; dot with remaining butter; sprinkle with lemon juice. Broil 2 inches from heat about 8 minutes or until easily flaked with a fork, but still moist. Melt cheese in milk until smooth. Place fish in a 12 by 8 by 2 inch baking dish. Top with spinach and pour cheese sauce over all. Broil 4 inches from heat until golden brown. Serves 6.

Sunday Roast Duck

1 6 lb. duck
Juice of 1 lemon
Salt and pepper
1 clove garlic

4 sprigs of parsley
1 whole apple
1 tsp. paprika
1 tbs. flour

Preheat oven to 400°. Wash and clean duck, removing as much fat as possible. Rub duck inside and out with lemon juice, salt, pepper and garlic. Place apple and parsley in cavity of duck. Place in hot oven uncovered for 15 minutes. Reduce heat to 350° and drain fat from pan. Sprinkle with paprika and flour and replace pan in oven and roast 20 minutes to the pound. Should be brown, crisp, and not greasy. Serves 4.

Lamb Shanks, Barbecued

4 to 6 lamb shanks
2 tbs. salad oil
1 large onion sliced thin
1 c. catsup
1 c. water

2 tsp. salt
3 tbs. Worcestershire sauce
¼ c. wine vinegar
2 tbs. brown sugar
2 tsp. dry mustard

Brown lamb shanks in salad oil. Combine remaining ingredients and pour over shanks. Simmer, covered, for 2 hours, basting several times during the cooking with the sauce. Remove cover and cook for 15 minutes longer. Makes 4 to 6 servings.

Broiled Swordfish Steaks

4 swordfish steaks	Juice of 1 lemon
1 clove minced garlic	2 tbs. chopped parsley
½ tsp. paprika	4 tbs. melted butter
Salt and pepper	

Preheat broiler. Place fish on aluminum foil on broiler pan. Sprinkle each steak with salt, pepper, garlic, paprika, lemon juice and parsley. Brush with melted butter and broil 3 inches away from heat for about 15 minutes, or until fish is firm and white. Serves 4.

Skewered Seafood Savoy

½ lb. cleaned shrimp	½ tsp. Tabasco sauce
½ lb. scallops	16 mushroom caps
Salt and pepper	12 pineapple cubes
1 tbs. Worcestershire sauce	¼ c. melted butter
1 tbs. lemon juice	1 tsp. chopped parsley
1 sm. minced onion	

Mix melted butter, seasonings, Worcestershire, Tabasco, lemon juice, onion and parsley. Marinate shrimp and scallops in mixture for 12 minutes. Alternate seafood and mushroom caps and pineapple on 6 inch skewers and place them in preheated broiler 3 inches from heat. Broil until golden brown. Serves 4.

Chicken Paprika

1 3 lb. frying chicken cut-up	3 tsp. paprika
3 tbs. corn oil	1 tsp. salt
2 onions, finely chopped	½ pt. sour cream

Heat oil in 12 inch skillet over moderate heat. Brown onions. Add paprika and chicken; sprinkle with salt. Cover; cook over very low heat for one hour until tender, turning after first half hour. Pour sour cream over chicken; heat. Serves 4.

Baked Ocean Perch

1 lemon, sliced thin	1 c. dairy sour cream
1 medium onion, sliced thin	1/8 tsp. salt
Salt and pepper	1/2 tsp. paprika
1 1/2 lbs. fillets of ocean perch	1 tsp. prepared mustard

Cover bottom of baking dish with lemon and onion slices. Sprinkle lightly with salt and pepper. Lay fillets on top. Cover. Bake 20 minutes in hot oven (400°); remove cover, combine remaining ingredients, spread over top. Place in broiler, 3 inches under heat, and broil until browned. Serves 4.

Stuffed Hamburgers

1 lb. lean ground beef	2 tsp. Worcestershire sauce
1 tsp. salt	1 onion, chopped fine
1 tsp. monosodium glutamate	4 thin slices tomato
1/8 tsp. pepper	

Mix ground beef with salt and pepper and monosodium glutamate. Divide into eight equal parts and make a thin patty of each part. Mix together the Worcestershire sauce and onion. On half the patties place a slice of tomato and a tablespoon of chopped onion. Top with a second patty and pinch edges together. Broil about 15 minutes, turning once. Serves 4.

Calf's Liver à la Venice

1 lb. calf's liver	Salt and pepper
2 large sweet onions	4 tbs. water
2 tbs. butter	4 lemon slices
1 tsp. chopped sweet basil	

Cut liver into one-inch squares. Peel and thinly slice onions; separate into rings. Melt butter in skillet; add onion rings. Sauté lightly for five minutes. Add liver, salt and pepper, and sweet basil to pan. Cook, stirring constantly, until liver chunks are brown on all sides. Add water and bring to a boil over high heat. Remove from heat immediately. Serve topped with lemon slice. Serves 4.

Corned Beef and Cabbage

4 lb. piece corned beef
4 whole cloves
1 bay leaf
1 clove garlic

1 tsp. monosodium glutamate
2 stalks celery, cut up
1 medium cabbage

Place corned beef in deep kettle and cover with cold water. Add remaining ingredients except cabbage and bring to boil. Reduce heat and simmer 5 minutes. Skim; then continue simmering for 3 to 4 hours, or until tender. Add hot water as needed. Cut cabbage into quarters, removing part of the core, and place on top of corned beef. Cover and cook until cabbage is tender, about 30 minutes. Serves 4.

Easy Sukiyaki

1 large onion cut into ¼ inch slices
4 young green onions with tops
½ lb. large fresh mushrooms
½ lb. rare roast beef from delicatessen

1 c. undiluted beef consommé
1 c. raw spinach, chopped
1 tsp. sugar
2 tbs. soy sauce

Separate onion into rings; chop green onions and tops into half-inch pieces. Wash and slice mushrooms. Place teflon skillet on medium flame. Place roast beef slices, onion rings, chopped green onion, and mushroom slices in skillet. Stir from time to time. Wash and chop spinach. Add chopped spinach, consommé, sugar and soy sauce to ingredients in skillet. Boil 2 minutes. Serves 4.

Hamburger Pie Italian Style

1 lb. lean ground beef
1 tsp. salt
½ tsp. pepper
1 c. canned tomatoes

½ c. shredded mozzarella cheese
2 tbs. chopped parsley
½ tsp. sweet basil
2 tbs. chopped onion

Mix ground beef with salt and pepper. Pat out in a 9-inch pie plate. Spread drained tomatoes over hamburger and sprinkle with the remaining ingredients. Bake in a 375° oven for 15 minutes. Cut in wedges. Serves 4.

Stuffed Tomatoes

4 large tomatoes
2 hard boiled eggs
1 can tuna fish
¼ tsp. pepper

1 tsp. capers
1 tbs. chopped parsley
3 tbs. mayonnaise

Cut tops off tomatoes and remove seeds and liquid. Mix together remaining ingredients and fill tomatoes with mixture. Chill and serve. Serves 4.

Eggs Piquante

5 chicken livers, diced fine
2 tbs. butter
2 tbs. sherry wine
2 tbs. warm water

4 eggs
1 tbs. butter
Salt and pepper
8 asparagus tips

Brown chicken livers lightly in butter; add wine and cook 5 minutes. Add warm water and cook 2 minutes longer. Break eggs into greased shallow baking dish, dot with butter; sprinkle with salt and pepper, and cook in 400° oven 10 minutes. Pour chicken livers over eggs, garnish with asparagus tips, bake 5 minutes longer. Serves 4.

Herbed Meat Balls

1 lb. lean ground beef
1 sm. green pepper, chopped
¼ tsp. thyme
1 sm. onion chopped

¼ tsp. paprika
½ tsp. marjoram
½ tsp. monosodium glutamate
Salt to taste

Combine all ingredients; shape into balls; and brown in teflon pan. Place in casserole dish. Add vegetable stock to drippings and simmer for 2 minutes. Pour over the meat balls and serve. Serves 4.

Italian Style Omelette

2 tbs. olive oil	4 eggs, lightly beaten
1 sm. zucchini, diced	3 tbs. grated Parmesan cheese
1 celery heart, diced	1 tsp. chopped basil
2 fresh tomatoes, peeled	1 tbs. olive oil
Salt and Pepper	

Brown zucchini and celery in oil in frying pan. Add cut up tomatoes, salt and pepper and cook for 15 minutes. Mix together in a bowl, eggs, cheese and basil and then pour over vegetables. Cook slowly using additional olive oil if necessary. Serves 4.

Chinese Chow Mein

½ lb. diced pork	1 tsp. fennel seeds
2 cups sliced Chinese cabbage	1 clove garlic
1 med. size onion, cut up	½ c. green pepper, sliced
½ cup water chestnuts	1 cup bean sprouts
½ cup bamboo shoots	3 tbs. soy sauce
½ cup mushrooms	

Sauté meat in teflon frying pan. Add vegetables and other ingredients and simmer gently until vegetables are cooked through. Add a little water if necessary to keep mixture moist. Serves 4.

Sweetbreads with Prosciutto

1 lb. lamb's sweetbreads	3 slices prosciutto
2 tbs. butter	2 tbs. Marsala
Salt and Pepper	

Place sweetbreads in cold water for 15 minutes. Change water, place in a saucepan and bring water to boiling point. Remove from heat, place again in cold water, drain, dry and remove skin. Melt butter in frying pan. Add sweetbreads and cook over brisk heat until golden brown. Add salt, pepper and prosciutto and cook 2 minutes. Add Marsala and cook 2 minutes longer. Serve immediately. Serves 4.

Veal Kidneys Napoli

4 veal kidneys
1 clove garlic
2 tbs. olive oil
¼ tsp. salt

⅛ tsp. pepper
2 filets of anchovies, chopped
1 tbs. chopped parsley
1 tsp. lemon juice

Slice kidneys as thin as possible and remove all fat. Brown garlic in oil over gentle heat, and when brown, remove garlic from pan. Add sliced kidneys, salt and pepper, and cook over high heat for 5 minutes. Add chopped anchovies, mix well and remove from heat. Add parsley and lemon juice and serve immediately. Serves 4.

Pork Chops in Wine Sauce

6 pork chops, cut very thick
½ tsp. salt.
⅛ tsp. pepper
1 tbs. olive oil

1 cup dry white wine
6 tbs. tomato paste
1 cup stock or water

Heat oil in large frying pan. Salt and pepper chops and place in pan. Brown well on both sides, keeping pan covered. When browned, pour off the fat and add the wine. Cover pan and simmer, turning chops occasionally. When the wine is nearly evaporated, add tomato paste and stock or water, well mixed, and cook another half hour or until chops are well done. Place chops on serving dish and pour the sauce over. Serves 6.

Braised Leg of Lamb

1 sm. leg of lamb
1 tbs. butter
1 large onion, sliced
1 large carrot, diced
2 stalks celery, diced

2 tbs. chopped parsley
1 tsp. salt
½ tsp. pepper
1 cup dry white wine
1 cup stock or water

Place leg of lamb in Dutch oven with butter and brown slowly on all sides. When brown, remove to a dish and keep warm. Place onion, carrot, celery and parsley in the Dutch oven and brown, adding a little water if necessary. When vegetables are brown, return meat to pot and pour over it any juices that drained from it while standing. Add salt, pepper and wine and cook until wine evaporates. Add stock, cover pot, and cook slowly for two hours or until meat is tender. Turn meat often during cooking. Remove meat to serving dish. Serves 6.

Spinach-Crab Soufflé

3 tbs. flour	4 eggs, separated
1 tsp. salt	1 cup chopped cooked fresh spin-
3 tbs. soybean oil	ach, well drained
¾ cup scalded milk	1 cup finely flaked crab meat
1 tsp. Worcestershire sauce	½ cup grated Cheddar cheese
⅛ tsp. liquid red-pepper seasoning	

Blend flour and salt into oil in medium-size saucepan; slowly stir in scalded milk, Worcestershire sauce, and red-pepper seasoning. Cook, stirring constantly, until mixture is thick. Cool. Beat egg whites in a medium-size bowl until they form soft peaks. Beat egg yolks until thick in a large bowl. Blend in cooled sauce, spinach, and crab meat; fold in beaten egg whites. Spoon into 8 six-ounce custard cups or individual soufflé dishes. Set cups in a large shallow pan for easy handling. Bake in hot oven (400°) for 20 minutes, or until puffy-firm and golden. Sprinkle cheese over top. Serve immediately. Serves 6.

Beefsteak Hunter Style

1 tbs. olive oil	2 tbs. sherry wine
1 porterhouse steak, 1½ inches thick	½ cup dry red wine
	½ clove garlic, minced
½ tsp. salt	½ tsp. fennel seeds
½ tsp. pepper	1 tbs. tomato puree

Heat oil in frying pan, add steak, cook on both sides until done to taste. Add salt and pepper; remove from pan and keep warm. Add sherry to pan and cook slowly, scraping bottom of pan with wooden spoon. Add red wine. Cook until wine has almost evaporated. Add garlic, fennel seeds and tomato puree; mix together well. Cook 1 minute longer. Pour over steak and serve. Serves 2.

Veal Birds

1 tbs. butter
1 tbs. olive oil
1 clove garlic
1 bay leaf
1 lb. thinly sliced veal cutlets, cut
  into 4-inch pieces

Salt and pepper
2 tsp. lemon juice
2 tbs. water
½ lb. mushrooms, sliced

Heat butter and oil with garlic and bay leaf in frying pan. Add veal seasoned with salt and pepper. Cook over high heat 3 minutes, turning meat twice during cooking. Remove veal and place on serving dish. Remove garlic and bay leaf from pan. Add lemon juice, water and mushrooms. Cook 2 minutes. Pour over veal and serve. Serves 4.

Swordfish Supreme

1½ lbs. swordfish
12 cherry tomatoes

3 tbs. low calorie Italian dressing
1 2-inch strip anchovy paste

Cut fish into one-inch cubes. Mix Italian dressing and anchovy paste together. Place fish cubes and tomatoes on skewers and brush with dressing mixture. Heat broiler and place skewers on aluminum foil under heat. Broil for seven minutes, turning often. Serve immediately. Serves 4.

Veal with Tarragon

1½ lb. veal, thinly sliced
1 tbs. butter
Juice of 1 lemon

Salt and pepper
3 tsp. fresh chopped tarragon
1 tsp. monosodium glutamate

Pound veal slices very thin and cut into serving pieces. Sauté in butter very quickly on both sides. Add lemon juice, salt and pepper to taste, tarragon and monosodium glutamate. Cook until tender, about ten minutes.

Pizza Pie Omelet

2 tbs. butter
2 medium-size tomatoes
4 Anchovies
4 eggs

8 thin slices mozzarella cheese
1 tsp. oregano
Salt and Pepper

Melt butter in frying pan. Slice tomato and place in pan. Cook over medium heat. Cut each anchovy in half and blot on paper toweling. Beat eggs in bowl. Pour eggs over tomato slices, Arrange anchovy pieces and cheese slices attractively on top of eggs. Sprinkle with oregano, salt and pepper. Place omelet under broiler one minute to melt cheese. Serve immediately. Serves 4.

Lamb Stew in Foil

4 double lamb chops	1 tsp. chopped rosemary
4 carrots, sliced	4 tbs. sherry
4 onions, sliced in rings	Salt, pepper, monosodium gluta-
4 stalks celery, sliced	mate

Cut four large squares of heavy aluminum foil. Rub chops with rosemary. Place one chop on each square of foil. Top each chop with equal quantities of vegetables. Season, and pour one tablespoon sherry over each portion. Fold foil so it is sealed and place on baking sheet. Bake in 300° oven for two hours. Serves 4.

Deviled Crabmeat and Mushrooms

1 can crabmeat	1 onion, chopped
1/2 lb. mushrooms	1 green pepper, chopped
1 envelope instant chicken broth mix	1 tsp. dry mustard
	3 tbs. light cream
1 cup water	1/2 tsp. tabasco sauce

Place sliced mushrooms, broth mix, water, onion, and green pepper in skillet. Cook over medium heat for three minutes. Stir once. Add mustard, cream, crabmeat and tabasco. Stir until smooth and fairly thick. Serve hot, either alone or on toast, if desired. Serves 4.

Savory Cream Cheese Custards

1 lg. pkg. cream cheese	1 tsp. fresh chopped rosemary
1/2 cup milk	Salt and pepper
1/2 cup light cream	1/2 tsp. paprika
1/4 cup sauterne wine	1 tsp. chopped tarragon
1 tbs. chopped chives	Butter
4 eggs	Fresh watercress

Thoroughly blend cheese, milk, cream and wine. Add chives, rosemary and tarragon. Beat eggs with salt, pepper, and paprika and combine with cheese mixture. Butter bottoms of six custard cups and fill. Set in pan of hot water. Bake in 325° oven until set. Serve from custard cups or turn out on serving dishes and garnish with watercress. Serves 6.

Capri Omelet

1 large green pepper, chopped	4 large eggs
2 medium-size tomatoes, chopped	Salt and pepper
2 tbs. butter	1 tsp. monosodium glutamate
1 clove garlic, minced	½ tsp. oregano

Melt butter in skillet. Add green pepper, tomatoes, and garlic. Sauté gently for 5 minutes. Beat eggs in a bowl and pour over mixture in skillet. Sprinkle with salt, pepper, monosodium glutamate and oregano. Stir gently with fork. Cook until eggs are set on bottom. Fold omelet and turn out onto serving plate. Serve hot. Serves 4.

Charcoal Broiled Shrimp

1½ lbs. shrimp, cleaned	1 tsp. garlic powder
Juice of 1 lemon	½ tsp. dried tarragon
8 large pimento-stuffed olives	Salt and pepper
4 tbs. low-calorie Italian dressing	Monosodium glutamate

Place all ingredients except shrimp and olives in a shallow casserole. Mix well. Add shrimp and olives and marinate for 1 hour, stirring and turning several times. Alternate olives and shrimp on skewers and broil over hot charcoal fire for three minutes on each side. Serve hot. Serves 4.

Deluxe Chicken Livers

1 lb. chicken livers	½ tsp. monosodium glutamate
4 strips bacon	Sprinkle of pepper
1 sm. onion, chopped	2 tbs. tomato paste
1 tbs. chopped parsley	3 tbs. milk
¼ tsp. thyme, basil and salt	

Chop chicken livers and bacon into one-inch squares. Sauté with onion, parsley, and spices for ten minutes. Drain off any excess bacon grease. Stir in tomato paste and milk. Cook one minute more. Serve hot. Serves 4.

Breast of Chicken with Artichokes

4 chicken breasts, skinned and boned
3 tbs. corn oil
1 c. artichoke hearts

3 tbs. whiskey
½ cup light cream
1 tsp. meat glaze
2 tbs. tomato paste

Melt butter in large skillet. Cut chicken into pieces and artichokes in half. Add to skillet, cooking over medium heat for ten minutes. Turn meat and artichokes, cook ten more minutes. Add whiskey. Light a match and hold near whiskey. As soon as whiskey is hot enough, it will ignite. When flame burns out, add remaining ingredients. Cook for one minute more or until sauce is fairly thick. Serve hot. Serves 4.

Beef Stroganoff

1½ lbs. filet of beef
Salt and pepper to taste
3 tbs. butter
1 medium onion, chopped

1 tbs. Gravy Master
½ cup sour cream
3 tbs. tomato paste

Cut beef into thin slices. Sprinkle with salt and pepper. Melt butter in skillet. Brown beef and onion in skillet. Remove from heat. Add Gravy Master to pan. Stir. Add half of sour cream. Stir. Add tomato paste. Stir. Add remainder of sour cream. Stir. Simmer over low heat, stirring constantly until sauce is steaming hot. Serve immediately. Serves 4.

Eggs Baked in Tomatoes

4 tomatoes, hollowed out and drained
4 eggs

Salt and Pepper
¼ tsp. thyme
2 tbs. water

Sprinkle inside of hollowed out tomato with salt. Break egg into tomato shell. Sprinkle with salt, pepper, and thyme. Put water in a small baking dish and place egg-filled tomato shells in dish. Bake for five minutes, or until egg is as firm as desired. Serve hot. Serves 4.

Sauced Tongue

3 tbs. butter
3 tsp. low-calorie maple syrup
1 tbs. grated yellow skin of lemon
1 bay leaf

½ cup beer
1 lb. sliced tongue (from delicatessen)

Melt butter in skillet. Add maple syrup. Remove from heat. Add lemon skin, bay leaf, and beer to skillet. Return to heat and cook over medium heat for two minutes. Add tongue slices and cook one minute more. Arrange tongue slices on serving plate, cover with sauce, and serve hot. Serves 4.

Old-Fashioned Meat Loaf

1 chopped onion
1 chopped green pepper
1 minced clove garlic
1½ lb. ground beef
1 egg

½ cup wheat germ
⅓ cup powdered milk
3 tbs. ground parsley
1 tsp. salt
⅛ tsp. each thyme and basil

Sauté lightly onion, green pepper and garlic. Remove from heat and add remainder of ingredients, mixing thoroughly. Pack into an oiled loaf pan and bake at 350° about 50 minutes. Serves 4.

Shrimp Scampi

1½ lbs. shrimp, cleaned
¼ cup olive oil
2 tbs. butter

½ tsp. salt
1 clove garlic
3 tbs. parsley, chopped

Heat olive oil and butter in skillet over high heat. Add shrimp and crushed garlic. Cook for about three minutes, stirring often. Add parsley and salt and cook for one minute more or until shrimp have turned pink; stir several times. Serve very hot. Serves 4.

Exotic Scrambled Egg Foo Young

3 strips lean bacon
½ lb. mushrooms, sliced
3 young green onions, sliced
1 can crabmeat

4 eggs
Salt and Pepper
½ tsp. monosodium glutamate

Cut bacon into pieces; cook over medium heat. When bacon is almost done, add sliced mushrooms and green onions. Stir. Cook over medium heat for two minutes. Beat eggs in a bowl. Add crabmeat to mixture in skillet. Cook for one minute more. Pour eggs over crabmeat mixture. Sprinkle with salt, pepper and monosodium glutamate. Stir over medium heat until egg is set but not dry. Serve hot. Serves 4.

Fillet of Flounder in Tomato-Wine Sauce

1½ lb. fillet of flounder
2 tbs. chopped parsley
1 sm. onion, chopped
3 tbs. butter
3 tbs. tomato paste
¼ tsp. garlic powder

1 tsp. sugar
1 tsp. prepared mustard
2 tsp. vinegar
Salt and pepper
¼ cup white wine
4 tbs. water

Place all ingredients except fish in a large skillet. Stir over medium heat until butter is melted. Add fish. Cook over medium heat for three minutes on each side. Carefully remove fish to serving plates. Serve immediately. Serves 4.

Celery Sticks Wrapped in Veal

4 4 oz. pieces of veal, cut thin
2 large celery stalks
2 oz. Swiss cheese, grated
2 tsp. catsup
2 tsp. soy sauce

1 tsp. sugar
¼ tsp. garlic powder
3 tbs. butter
Salt and pepper
½ cup undiluted beef consommé

Flatten and spread open veal slices. Wash celery and slice into sticks no thicker than matchsticks. Place grated Swiss cheese, catsup, half of soy sauce, sugar, and garlic powder into small bowl. Mash with tablespoon until this forms a paste. Wrap the paste around half of the celery sticks and place these on veal pieces (one pack of celery sticks on each piece of veal). Roll veal around celery sticks. Secure with toothpicks. Place skillet on medium-high heat. Sprinkle lightly with salt. When pan is hot, place butter and veal in center. Fry until brown. Carefully loosen veal, turn over and repeat process until entire veal roll is lightly browned. Measure consommé and remaining soy sauce into frying pan. Add remainder of celery sticks. Boil for one minute. Serve hot with loose celery sticks at the side or on top of the veal roll along with any sauce remaining in pan. Serves 4.

SALADS

Shrimp-Orange Salad

3 medium oranges, peeled, cut
  into bite-size pieces
½ c. sliced celery
½ c. sliced ripe olives

½ lb. cooked shrimp, cleaned
2 tbs. chopped onion
¼ tsp. salt
Citrus Honey Dressing

Combine orange pieces, celery, olives, shrimp, chopped onion, and salt. Blend with a little Citrus Honey Dressing to moisten. Chill. Serve in lettuce cup on individual salad plates with more dressing if desired. Serves 6.

Citrus Honey Dressing

¼ c. honey
½ c. mayonnaise
1 tbs. grated orange peel

3 tbs. orange juice
1 tbs. lemon juice
¼ tsp. paprika

Combine all ingredients, blending well. Chill.

Salmon Banana Salad

½ c. canned pineapple pieces
3 bananas, diced
1 c. salmon, skinned and boned
½ c. diced celery

¼ tsp. salt
2 tbs. mayonnaise
Lemon slices

Drain pineapple well. Mix together with bananas. Add salmon and stir in remaining ingredients. Serve on lettuce, garnished with lemon slices.

Fruit Salad Provincale

1 c. diced canned pineapple
2 sliced bananas
1 orange, peeled and cut into pieces
2 apples, peeled, cored and diced
4 walnut halves

6 lettuce leaves
½ c. heavy cream
½ tsp. sugar
⅛ tsp. salt
1 tbs. lemon juice

Mix fruit together. Line fruit bowl with lettuce leaves and place fruit in center. Mix cream, sugar, salt and lemon juice and pour over fruit. Chill before serving. Serves 4. (Garnish with walnut halves.)

Cucumber Salad

2 cucumbers
¼ tsp. salt
½ tsp. monosodium glutamate

½ c. sour cream
1 tsp. chopped chives

Peal and thinly slice cucumbers. Add spices, sour cream and chives and toss gently. Serves 4.

Molded Apple Salad

1 envelope unflavored gelatin
¼ c. cold water
½ c. boiling water
1 c. apple or pineapple juice

2 Delicious apples, grated
1 tbs. honey
½ c. chopped nuts

Dissolve gelatin in cold water, then add the boiling water. Cool. Add the fruit juice. Add apples and remaining ingredients and pour into a greased mold. Refrigerate until set. Unmold on lettuce leaves and top with mayonnaise if desired. Serves 4.

Savory Pear-Cheese Salad

2 large Bartlett pears
1/4 c. soft process American cheese
3 tbs. cream cheese
1/4 tsp. milk
1/2 tsp. lemon juice
Lettuce
French dressing, if desired

Cut pears in 1/4 inch lengthwise slices. Remove cores and seeds. Mix cheeses with milk and lemon juice until smooth. Arrange pear slices on lettuce and spoon some cheese mixture on each serving. Serve with dressing if desired. Serves 4.

Sunday Cottage Cheese Salad

1 envelope unflavored gelatin
1/4 c. cold water
1/2 c. boiling water
1 pt. cottage cheese
1 tbs. chopped chives
1/2 red pepper, chopped
1/2 green pepper, chopped
1 tsp. salt
1 tsp. dried basil
1/2 tsp. monosodium glutamate

Dissolve gelatin in cold water, then add the boiling water. Add all remaining ingredients in order. Pour into an oiled salad mold and refrigerate until set. Unmold on salad greens and serve with mayonnaise if desired.

Chinese Shrimp Salad

1 lb. fresh shrimp, cleaned and
    shelled
1 tsp. salt
1/2 c. French dressing
3 tbs. teriyaki sauce
2 tbs. lemon juice
1 c. bean sprouts, drained
1 carrot, shredded
4 hard cooked eggs, sliced
1 c. diagonally sliced celery
1 onion, sliced and separated into
    rings

Cook shrimp in boiling water for five minutes. Drain well. Mix French dressing, teriyaki sauce and lemon juice in a pie plate; add shrimps, turn to coat well. Chill, stirring occasionally. Place shrimp, bean sprouts, carrot, egg slices and celery and onion slices on lettuce leaves. Drizzle dressing from shrimps over all. Serves 6.

German Kraut Salad

1 lb. sauerkraut	1 large carrot, sliced thin
1 tbs. vegetable oil	2 large red apples
1 tbs. minced onion	1 tbs. cider vinegar
½ tsp. salt	Lettuce leaves

Drain sauerkraut well; pat dry between sheets of paper toweling. Combine with vegetable oil, onion, salt and about three quarters of the carrot slices in a medium-size bowl; toss lightly to mix. Chill. Pare, core and dice one of the apples. Toss with vinegar in small bowl. Add to sauerkraut mixture. Spoon into lettuce-lined bowl. Quarter remaining apple; core and slice thin. Stand slices in a ring around edge on salad; pile remaining carrot slices in center. Serves 6.

Eggplant Salad

1 medium-size eggplant	1 clove garlic, minced
1 large cucumber	1 tsp. lemon juice
1 c. diced celery	1 tsp. salt
⅓ c. sliced stuffed olives	½ tsp. sugar
1 sm. onion, chopped	¼ tsp. paprika
½ c. sour cream	2 hard-cooked eggs

Wash eggplant; place in a shallow pan. Bake in very hot oven (450°) for 20 minutes or until tender. Cool until easy to handle, then pare, cut into ½ inch thick slices, and cube slices. Place in a medium-size bowl. Pare cucumber and slice thin. Add to eggplant with celery, olives and onion. Blend sour cream, garlic, lemon juice, salt, sugar, and paprika in a small bowl. Pour over eggplant mixture; toss lightly. Spoon into lettuce-lined bowl; arrange eggs cut into wedges on top. Serves 6.

Pear and Pineapple Salad

1 large ripe pear	½ c. yogurt
8 slices canned pineapple	⅛ tsp. nutmeg

Pare pear. Stand on blossom end and cut lengthwise into 16 thin slices. Remove core where necessary. Place two pear slices on a lettuce-lined plate; top each with a pineapple slice. Combine yogurt and nutmeg in a cup; spoon 1 tablespoon over each salad.

DESSERTS

Honey Pumpkin Pudding

2 c. cooked or canned pumpkin   ½ tsp. salt
2 c. milk   1 tsp. cinnamon
1 c. honey   ½ tsp. ginger
2 eggs

Mix ingredients in order given. Beat well. Pour into individual custard cups or baking dishes and place these in a large pan of hot water. Bake in 350° oven for one hour. Serves 6.

Drifting Island

1½ c. milk   3 eggs, separated
1 tbs. sugar   1 tsp. vanilla
⅛ tsp. salt   5 tbs. sugar

Scald milk in saucepan; add 1 tbs. sugar and the salt and stir until sugar dissolves. Beat egg yolks slightly. Add milk mixture to egg yolks. Cook over hot water until thickened, stirring constantly. Cool. Add vanilla. Pour into shallow serving dish and chill. Set oven for 325°. Beat egg whites stiff. Add remaining sugar gradually, beating constantly. Grease 9-inch pie plate; place over a 9-inch layer cake pan almost filled with hot water. Put meringue mixture into pie plate; swirl top with back of spoon. Bake 15 minutes. Remove meringue with broad spatula; slip onto custard. Serves 6.

Whipped Fruit

2 egg whites   1 c. fruit pulp (crushed berries,
¼ c. powdered sugar   peaches, applesauce, prune, or
                                      apricot pulp)

Beat egg whites until stiff. Add sugar gradually while beating. Fold in fruit. Pile in sherbet glasses; chill. Serves 4.

Nut Cake

1 c. finely chopped walnuts   1 tsp. vanilla
7 eggs separated   pinch of salt
1 c. brown sugar

Beat egg whites until very stiff and dry. Set aside. Beat egg yolks
and sugar together until creamy; add nut meats gradually, then salt
and vanilla. Fold this mixture into the whites carefully and bake in
an ungreased tube pan for 1 hour at 325°. Invert pan to cool as for
angel cake.

No-Cook Applesauce

2 c. raw apples, quartered, cored   Pinch salt
½ c. raisins   1 tbs. honey
Pinch nutmeg

Put ¼ c. water in blender and cut apples in and reduce to pulp.
Add raisins, seasonings and honey and run another few seconds. Pile
in sherbet glasses. Serves 4.

Peach Melba

1 box (10 oz.) frozen raspberries,   1½ tsp. cornstarch
    thawed   3 large peaches, peeled and
⅓ c. low calorie currant jelly   halved
⅛ tsp. salt   1 qt. vanilla ice cream

Mash raspberries in saucepan and add jelly and salt. Bring to a boil,
stirring until jelly is melted. Blend cornstarch with 1 tbs. water and
stir this mixture into jelly mixture. Cook, stirring, until clear and
slightly thickened. Cool, then chill. When ready to serve, put 1 peach
half, rounded side down, in each of 6 sherbet glasses. Cover with scoop
of ice cream; top with sauce.

Jellied Wine

1 envelope unflavored gelatin   1 c. rosé wine
⅓ c. sugar   ¼ c. sherry
2 tbs. lemon juice   Whipped cream (if desired)

Mix gelatin and sugar. Add ½ c. boiling water and stir until gelatin dissolves. Add next 3 ingredients and blend well. Pour into four 4-ounce molds and chill until firm. Unmold and serve with whipped cream, if desired. Makes 4 servings.

Fruit Medley

2 tbs. lime juice
½ c. honey
3 peaches, peeled and sliced

3 apricots, peeled and sliced
2 plums, sliced
Mint sprigs

Mix lime juice and honey and pour over peaches and apricots. Put in serving dishes. Arrange a few plum slices on each serving and decorate with mint. Serves 4.

Melon Delight

2 cups melon balls
2 navel oranges, cut up
2 bananas, sliced

1 tbs. sugar
1 tbs. lemon juice
⅓ cup flaked coconut

Mix first 5 ingredients and chill. Top with a sprinkling of coconut. Serves 6.

Strawberry Circle

1 envelope unflavored gelatin
½ c. cold water
2 cups fresh strawberries, hulled

1 tsp. lemon juice
2 egg whites
¼ c. sugar

In a small saucepan, soften gelatin in water and heat slowly, stirring constantly until gelatin dissolves; remove from heat and cool. Wash and crush berries; stir in gelatin mixture and lemon juice and chill until thickened. Beat egg whites until double in volume and then beat in sugar, 1 tbs. at a time until meringue stands in firm peaks. Fold into thickened strawberry mixture and spoon into a 4-cup tube mold. Chill until firm. When ready to serve, unmold onto a medium-size plate. Serve plain or with whipped cream. Serves 6.

Cantaloupe DeLuxe

1 banana   2 tsp. sugar
4 tbs. sour cream   1 medium-size cantaloupe

Mash banana in a bowl until quite smooth. Add sour cream and sugar to banana and mix thoroughly. Refrigerate. Peel cantaloupe and cut into cubes. Add cantaloupe to sour cream mixture and toss lightly until covered with cream. Serves 4.

Apple-Pear Betty

3 medium-size apples   1 cup low calorie pear slices
1 tbs. butter   3 tbs. low calorie maple syrup
½ tsp. cinnamon

Peel, core and slice apples. Melt butter in skillet and add apples and cinnamon. Cook over medium heat until apple slices are slightly browned, stirring occasionally. Drain pears and add to apple mixture along with maple syrup. Stir gently for one minute. Turn onto serving dish. Serve warm or cool, with whipped cream, if desired. Serves 4.

Minted Pineapple with Coconut

2 cups low-calorie pineapple,   2 tsp. grated coconut
  chilled   mint leaves
2 tsp. creme de menthe

Drain pineapple and arrange in sherbet glasses. Dribble creme de menthe over pineapple and sprinkle with grated coconut. Tuck fresh mint leaves here and there in glass, and serve ice cold. Serves 4.

Strawberry Yogurt

2 cups fresh strawberries   ½ tsp. vanilla extract
½ cup plain yogurt   4 tsp. sugar
½ tsp. almond extract

Wash and drain strawberries. Gently mix yogurt, extracts and sugar in bowl. Add strawberries and again, mix gently. Serve cold in sherbet glasses. Serves 4.

Creamy Rhubarb

1 bunch rhubarb
2 tbs. brown sugar
Grated lemon peel

¼ tsp. cinnamon
2 eggs, separated

Wash and cut rhubarb into small pieces. Cook with a little water; sieve. Add 1 tbs. brown sugar, grated lemon peel and cinnamon and allow to cool. Beat egg yolks with 1 tbs. brown sugar and add to cooled rhubarb. Beat the egg whites until stiff and fold into rhubarb mixture. Serves 4.

Baked Honey Pears

8 low-calorie pear halves
¼ c. lemon juice
½ c. honey

1 tsp. cinnamon
2 tbs. butter

Arrange pears in shallow buttered baking dish. Pour lemon juice and honey over pears. Sprinkle with cinnamon and dot with butter. Bake in 350° oven. Serve hot with cream if desired. Serves 4. (Peaches may be substituted for pears.)

Honey Custard

¼ tsp. salt
3 eggs, slightly beaten
¼ cup honey

2 cups milk, scalded
nutmeg

Add salt to eggs. Beat eggs slightly. Add honey to milk and add this mixture slowly to egg mixture. Pour into custard cups. Top with a few gratings of nutmeg. Set custard cups in pan of hot water and bake in 325° oven for about 40 minutes.

Zabaglione

4 egg yolks
4 tbs. honey

4 tbs. dry red wine

Place ingredients over medium direct heat and bring to gentle boil, beating constantly until thick and fluffy. Place in sherbert glasses. May be served warm or cold. Serves 4.

Aruba Whip

1 egg white
1 medium avocado

1½ tbs. lemon juice
1½ tbs. honey
whipped cream

Whip white of 1 egg until stiff. Add to it a cut-up ripe avacado. Mix together. Add 1½ tbs. lemon juice and 1½ tbs. honey. Beat all together. Put into wine glasses and top with dab of whipped cream. Serves 4.

Heavenly Baked Bananas

6 bananas
½ lb. cream cheese
3 tbs. butter

3 tbs. brown sugar
Cinnamon to taste
1 cup plain yogurt

Halve the peeled bananas lengthwise and brown lightly in butter. Butter a pie plate and place six halves on the bottom. Cream sugar, cream cheese and cinnamon and spread half of the amount on the six banana halves. Place remaining bananas on top and spread with the balance of the cheese mixture. Pour yogurt on top and bake for 20 minutes in 375° oven. Serves 6.

Fancy Brown Rice Pudding

⅓ c. brown rice
3½ c. milk
¼ c. lt. brown sugar
1 tbs. gelatin

3 tbs. cold water
1 tsp. almond extract
1 tsp. vanilla
½ c. cream, whipped

Wash rice and cook it in the top of a double boiler, covered, until tender (about an hour), stirring occasionally. Add the sugar and the gelatin which has soaked 3 minutes in the cold water. When the mixture is cold, add the extracts and whipped cream. Chill before serving. Serves 6.

Miracle Step Five

Review the calorie limits for each meal. Understand the protein "barometer." Go through your own recipe file and select a number that do not include sugars, starches and other carbohydrate-heavy ingredients. Check the 100 recipes in this chapter and plan to include your favorites soon. Hold portions down to below normal on the more sophisticated dishes. Go "wild" if you wish on the eat-all-you-want vegetables. Remember the advantages to your body of "fresh" and "local" foods.

6

How to Select Miracle Foods

The ban on cyclamates, besides halting the use of a potentially dangerous chemical, has had an interesting and valuable side effect.

Dieters, including diabetics, who have felt a sense of security in eating a candy bar just because it did not contain sugar, have now paused to reconsider. A dietetic candy bar can have as many, if not more, calories than a regular candy bar. Diabetics are on a calorie-limited diet just as are ordinary weight-conscious dieters. Either can ill afford to consume 300 calories of fat and starch— 300 calories without protein, minerals or vitamins.

These are empty, dead calories.

There are foods that are bursting with calories come alive. They are the Miracle Diet foods.

A dieter is obviously doing his body an injustice to waste his limited calorie intake on empty calories. He, even more than the non-dieter, must make every calorie count.

So, you say, proteins it is with some fruits and vegetables every day.

Fine, I say, but that is not enough. You may get by, but you won't see any miracles happen.

I want you to feel better while you are losing weight than you ever felt before.

I want you to be more vigorous and energetic, more youthful and radiant, more attractive and successful.

I don't want you to feel diet-listless, act diet-sluggish, and look diet-worn. I want you to radiate vitality and awareness as the pounds drop away.

That's the miracle!

Foods That Pack a Nutritional Wallop for Weight Control

To accomplish this miracle, it is not enough to eat steak just because it is not a candy bar. True, you are making a wise choice between the two. But the limits of your choice are far more extensive than that.

You would be taking just as large a nutritional step forward to choose liver instead of steak. Not only do four ounces of liver contain fewer calories than four ounces of steak, but four ounces is a more satisfying portion (we seldom can stop short of eight ounces of steak but, for some, three ounces of liver is quite adequate) and it contains far more nutrients.

Our number one food is protein. But there are proteins that excel other proteins. To bring about the miracle of the Miracle Diet we must be discriminating in our choice.

How do we discriminate?

Which proteins are best?

Which should we avoid?

Unfortunately, the science of nutrition does not provide us with easy, ready-made answers. We have only some broad guidelines to go by.

I want to give you these guidelines because you need to garner all the knowledge you can in order to vary your Miracle Diet fare in a way that will magnify, not minimize, the miracle.

Guideline No. 1—Fish Gets Priority over Meat

Fish is a valuable food. The sea, and most fresh water sources, are brimming with minerals. And fish is low in calories:

CALORIE CONTENT OF A 4-OUNCE PORTION OF COMMON FISH

Frogs Legs	44	Croaker	84
Codfish	48	Lobster	84
Oysters	50	Scallops	84
Flounder	64	Carp	93
Muscles	64	Finnan Haddie	96
Sole	76	Haddock	96
Clams	76	Catfish	98
Pike	80	Bass	99
Red Snapper	81	Crabmeat	99
Shrimp	82	Tuna	146
Perch	82	Canned Salmon	164
Porgy	84	Canned Sardines	167

Now compare the above with these typical meats:

CALORIE CONTENT OF A 4-OUNCE PORTION OF COMMON MEATS

Veal	144	Beef	215
Poultry	166	Pork Chop	222
Liver	170	Lamb (leg)	265
Pork Loin	209		

We can see at a glance that a four-ounce portion of fish is likely to cost us fewer calories than a similar portion of meat. Most types of fish are even more nutritious than meat.

I rate shellfish high in nutrients. However, I doubt if anyone can tell you whether flounder has an edge over codfish or whether pike is as good or better than perch.

Certainly they are all ahead of meat. However, here again, with liver as rich as it is in vitally needed minerals and vitamins, do you rate liver above or below fish?

I have no scientific data, so I would not want to debate the issue, but I would favor calf's liver, beef liver, chicken liver and other organ meats such as heart and kidney over even fish.

We are now getting down to a matter of taste and a degree of miracle. As long as you satisfy your taste with these valuable foods, you are eligible for the benefits in youth and brimming good health that come with such vital foods.

Guideline No. 2—Liver and Other Organ Meats Get Priority over Beef, Pork, and Lamb

Vary your menu. Include organ meats. Include fish. Enjoy poultry occasionally. Limit lamb, pork and beef to two or three times a week. Veal is a better choice than steak (smaller portion needed, and far fewer calories consumed).

Protein is also found abundantly in milk, cheese and eggs. Any priorities here?

Skimmed milk is skimmed only of fat. All the protein remains.

8 ounces of whole milk contains 140 calories.

8 ounces of skimmed milk contains 75 calories.

1 tablespoon of dried skimmed milk contains 24 calories.

Naturally, I vote for skimmed milk. And I prefer fresh skimmed milk to the dried variety, naturally.

Now as to cheese:

CALORIE CONTENT OF A 4-OUNCE PORTION OF COMMON CHEESES

Cottage Cheese (skimmed)	101	American	285
Cottage Cheese (regular)	140	Liederkranz	298
Camembert	206	Muenster	301
Fondeau	210		

As you can guess, cottage cheese gets my vote for more bounce to the ounce. I doubt if anybody can rate one cheese above another nutrition-wise, so:

Guideline No. 3—Cottage Cheese Is to Be Favored over Other Cheeses. These Other Cheeses Should Be Kept to Very Modest Portions

I would go a step further and say that regular cheese should be scheduled no more than twice weekly.

As to eggs, they are a fine meal (2) or snack (1). They are 75 calories each. When frying or scrambling use a teflon pan and a minimum of butter, margarine or oil. The whites of egg are pure protein. The yolks contain some fat. Be so guided in using them in recipes. Nutrition-wise, eggs rate near the top of the list.

Why Proteins?

I've talked a lot about the importance of protein to the body, but now let me be a bit more specific. If you are going to support protein in the election of food, you need to know its "inside" story in order to vote for it.

Your entire basic body is largely protein. Look at yourself in the mirror. Your skin, hair and muscles are protein. The base of your bones is protein. Your internal organs, including your brain, are protein.

Muscles are among the first parts of your body to show a lack of protein. I remember a 55-year-old woman who came to me all stooped over like she was an octogenarian. She just could not stand up straight because her muscles were not strong enough to hold her erect. In the process of losing weight on a high protein diet, her posture began to improve. In three short weeks she was holding her head high and her spirits were soaring. She thought it was because she had ten less pounds to carry. I told her about protein.

Of course, protein was helping this woman in other ways, too. True, her muscles regained their natural elasticity and strength, but her hair and nails also regained a resiliency. Her protein-hungry skin became more radiant and "alive." Her old fatigue, caused by protein deficiency, was replaced by abundant energy as the body's ability to produce the enzymes necessary to turn food into energy was restored.

Digestion suffers when one's posture is bad. Muscular walls and stomach muscle ligaments become flabby. The stomach and intestine walls which act as muscles on many foods, with digestive secretions and enzymes, do not function well when there is a protein deficiency. You can also imagine what can happen to the delicate balanced position of stomach, transverse bowel and colon.

A protein lack shows up, too, in the blood, guardian against disease. Antibodies are not produced in sufficient quantity. The white blood cells known as phagocytes are no longer in sufficient number to digest invaders.

I could go on and on. Waste materials are not properly removed. Blood will not clot properly. The brain will not function clearly. The acid-alkaline balance of the body will become unregulated. Excess poison-laden fluids will build up to bloat the body. Etc., etc., etc.

Your kitchen is your voting booth. Protein is a candidate for your vote. How will you cast your ballot?

You Can Be Overweight and Under Nourished

The American people have been called the best fed people in the world. They are, perhaps, too well fed, because 20 to 30 percent are decidedly overweight—that is, 20 percent or more above their desirable weight.

Yet, even these overweight people contribute to statistics on malnutrition. Some have anemia, indicating an iron deficiency. Some have a fluoride deficiency leading to tooth decay and osteoporosis (bone problems). Some have a susceptibility to arteriosclerosis due to not enough polyunsaturated fat and too much saturated fat and cholesterol.

Imagine what happens when these people go on a starvation diet, or a grapefruit diet, or a toast and tea diet. Certainly they will develop even greater shortages of what they are lacking, and possibly incur symptoms of serious trouble.

Since there are some 50 nutrients that the body needs, most diets throttle the intake of almost all of these. Little wonder the body makes its needs known through the only way it can—frequent hunger and lack of energy.

The trick is to pack more nutrients into less food.

How About That Evening Martini?

May dieters drink? I say yes—in moderation and only non-carbohydrate drinks. Certainly that evening martini or two is not going to cut too harshly into nutritional calories. However, beer is out. Sweet wines and mixed drinks are taboo.

There are no carbohydrates in scotch, rye, bourbon, gin, vodka or very dry wines. However, there are calories and not very nourishing calories. Whatever they are displacing because of the calorie limit on total intake, those foods are worth more in nutrition.

I have heard talk recently[1] about whether distillers should lace their liquor with vitamins. There has also been talk about public bars being required to place bowls of vitamin pills alongside the peanuts.

Though rejected as impractical, these ideas point up the fact that medical science recognizes that alcohol contributes not to nutrition of the human body, but to its malnutrition.

The most immediate and direct way that alcohol induces nutritional deficiency is that it displaces food. Drinkers eat less. They also tend to eat more carbohydrates. They also develop a progressive depletion of the B-complex vitamin known as Thiamine. Affected by this are the gait, the memory, and the general nervous system.

Again I say, the one or two martinis are OK. The occasional dry sherry is fine. They are not helping the miracle, but neither are they preventing it.

If you understand just how alcohol impedes the process of nutrition, then you are more likely to pay alcohol the respect it deserves, to approach it with moderation, and to make some sacrifice in the interests of a healthier, more slender, and vital *you*.

The Truth About Food Preservatives and Food Coloring

Recently a Wisconsin doctor discovered why he had been experiencing severe attacks of pain in his joints that had persisted on and off for several years. Refusing to accept the suggestion of others that it might be rheumatism, he kept records of everything he ate to see if he could find some hint of the cause.

He was soon rewarded for his effort. He found that the pains occurred whenever he ate certain foods such as frozen vegetables, smoked salmon, barbecued chicken, tomato juice and others. These

---

[1] 9th International Congress of Neurology.

foods, he discovered, all had some sodium nitrate added to preserve color. It was this chemical that was causing his pains.

Most chemicals used to preserve food cause no obvious difficulties to the human body. If they did, they would soon be out-
lawed by the Food and Drug Administration. But they add nothing in the way of nutrition and can cause acute problems with
some people, like the Wisconsin doctor, who are allergic or sensitive to them.

There is no known nutritional value to the sodium benzoate
used so frequently as a preservative, or calcium disodium, or any
of the other long tongue-twisters that appear on food packaging.

They may even have a negative value for many people—too
little to be significant, too minor to measure—but nevertheless on
the side of the scales that weigh against vitality, not for it.

I'm on dangerous ground. But I'm in good company.

Nutritionists like Carlton Fredericks and Adele Davis have long
beat the drums against chemical fertilizers and chemical preservatives and have incurred the wrath of those interests whose toes
were being stepped on.

However, today the shouts of "faddist" and "crack-pot" are
being stilled as thousands of professionals join the ranks of those
who see the error of arsenic, DDT, cyclamates, and maybe many
other chemical sprays and additives heretofore thought harmless.

This is another reason why "fresh local" is to be preferred over
"fresh distant," "fresh distant" over frozen, and frozen over
canned.

Foods with Life in Them

Enough about the forces that stifle nutrition and vitality. Let's
get positive.

There are many foods that bear the essence of life and which
transfer that essence to us when we consume them. We feel it
and show it as it reinforces our vitality and exuberance.

Green is the color of nature's living plants. Green is everywhere
in nature. When a plant dies, the green disappears.

Fresh living edible greens bear the essence of life within them.

They are nourishing and rejuvenating. You know them as well as I do.

You may know spinach and cabbage better than mustard greens and dandelion greens.

You may know lettuce and watercress better than turnip greens and beet greens.

You may know celery and broccoli better than kale and collards.

What you are familiar with is more likely to be acceptable to you than the unknown. I say go to it, as long as you include greens in your menu and benefit from their valuable essences.

However, whenever you try something new you expand your taste horizons. *You also broaden your base of good nutrition.* Make it a "habit" to try something new every week.

Have you ever tried Chinese cabbage? Artichokes? Brussels sprouts? Chicory? Chard? How about some raw green peppers in your salad tonight?

Grains That Nourish the Whole Body

Bread has been called the staff of life. White bread is consumed in the millions of loaves a day in the United States. Staff of life maybe—like a crutch to lean on—but not the stuff of life.

When wheat is processed for white bread a score of nutrients go down the drain. Recently, bakeries have admitted to this and attempted to rectify the matter by restoring several nutrients. The so-called "enriched" product is far better than its white predecessor, but still a long way from an unprocessed whole wheat bread.

Whole wheat flour has 10 percent fewer calories than white flour, but it has:

30 percent more protein
250 percent more calcium
300 percent more phosphorus
300 percent more iron
Nearly 10 times as much B_1 thiamin
More than twice as much B_1 riboflavin
Nearly 5 times as much B_1 niacin

It follows that you are doing yourself a giant nutritional favor to favor whole wheat over processed white. Make it a slice of whole wheat toast next time.

The same applies to rice. Brown rice, while slightly lower in calories than white rice, has:

50 percent more calcium
125 percent more phosphorus
Nearly triple the iron
Four times as much B_1 thiamin
And about twice as much riboflavin and niacin

Obviously, if we are going to include rice for breakfast or as a side dish, we are far better off with brown rice.

Though not a grain, flour made from the soybean is a standout. When you compare it to other flours, it is by far the highest in protein and iron and the B_1 vitamins. Too bad it is hard to appreciate taste-wise, but it certainly is a good substitute in cooking.

A by-product of enriched flour is wheat germ. This is the embryo of the wheat kernel. Rich in Vitamins B_1, B_2 and E, and in phosphorus, potassium and other minerals, it is delicious when added to breakfast cereals.

As you can expect, the germ of life is contained in many edible seeds. Interest has been mounting yearly in sunflower seeds, sesame seeds, and pumpkin seeds. Mexico and Russia are the top producers of sunflower oil recognized throughout South America and Europe for its nutritional value.

Many families now keep a bowl of these seeds within easy reach for healthful and tasteful snacking.

For centuries the followers of Yoga have sought healthful eating habits that provide the body with an abundance of natural nutrients despite a comparatively frugal diet. Their success has encouraged the spread of the practice of Yoga beyond the boundaries of India to all corners of the world.

Yogis favor whole foods in their cooking—foods which have not had their chemistry altered by removal of living essences and minerals. White flour and white sugar, bleached in the sulphuric acid, are replaced with the whole grain unprocessed forms. Although they make use of wine flavors in cooking in such a way that the alcohol is cooked away, they do not drink alcoholic beverages.

Yogis find great food value in such foods as wheat germ and bean sprouts. They produce the bean sprouts in their homes by placing mung beans between wet blotters. In two to three days they have a harvest of sprouts, bursting with the essence of life.

They cook in small amounts of water or oil to prevent the loss of minerals. They often drink the cooking water or use it as soup stock. They make frequent use of such flours as barley, millet, rye, potato, soy and rice as substitutes for wheat.

Live Longer with Miracle Diet Foods

When I mention the advantages of yogurt, or of honey as a sweetener instead of sugar, or of blackstrap molasses or yeast, many people are unmoved. Yogurt does not "turn them on." Blackstrap molasses "leaves them cold" and they "couldn't care less" about yeast. As to liver, greens, whole wheat, skimmed milk—forget it.

Yet before they leave my office, their curiosity is aroused, and their motivation to try these miracle diet foods is charged up. How? By simple reminders of what these foods are doing for people. I hope to interest and motivate you, too, by spelling out here and now some simple nutritional facts of life:

You will live longer if you weigh less. The insurance companies know just how much longer with how much fewer pounds. At 35 years of age, for instance, a man who is 25 percent overweight for a number of years takes 12 years off his life expectancy. A woman at that age and 25 percent overweight for a number of years is taking seven years off her life expectancy. For a man of 40 who has been 60 percent overweight, the day has about come according to the record, and for his overweight counterpart in the female sex, a life expectancy of 77 years is reduced to 55 years.

Nourishing foods change your life. Many people who eat "normally" (high carbohydrate, low protein) are bored with life. They have no interest in new people, new experiences, new ideas. They are not to blame. What they eat is to blame. A shift in diet away from "dead" sugary and starchy foods and toward life-renewing proteins and "vital" foods can change you from a listless person and make you come alive with a new exuberance and with a renewed interest in life.

Nourishing foods speed weight loss. When you replace fatty sugars and starches with foods that are rich in body-building nutrients, you are never as hungry. You feel better and look better as you lose weight. Your diet becomes less doomed to end soon and you less doomed to regain lost weight and then some. You stay slender.

Vital foods make you look younger. If we are what we eat, then it is obvious that eating fresh, alive foods and cell-building proteins can have dramatic effects on our state of health and on our youthfulness. "Dead" foods can clog your system and the resulting back-up can slow the action of all your vital organs. This spells old age. Give your body the foods it needs to do its work and the traffic moves easily, vital organs function better. And that spells youth. Following is a letter from one of my clients:

> Just a line to let you know that there has been an unexpected bonus to the diet you gave me. We never discussed it, but I am sure you noticed that my complexion was not all it could be. Well, it must have been caused by some deficiency in what I was eating because the blemishes have cleared up considerably. Needless to say, this has been great for my morale. . . .

Vital foods can improve your personality and intelligence. Depleted diets can cause anemia. This can reduce the amount of oxygen that reaches the brain, causing fuzzy thinking and indecision. Protein shortages can result in the brain cannibalizing itself —important brain cells survive on the protein of less needed brain cells. Vital foods prevent this—keep you at your peak intelligence and awareness.

I mentioned honey as a sweetener. In addition to its fruit sugar and grape sugar (very little cane sugar), honey contains some "extras" seldom found in processed sugar. It has dextrins and gums and a number of minerals, albeit in minute quantities: iron, copper, magnesium, aluminum, sulfur, silica, manganese, sodium and phosphorus.

Sugar, and honey, require many of the B vitamins for metabolism. Honey supplies a portion of these while sugar does not.

Honey contains a small amount of vitamins. These include about $\frac{1}{25}$ of the thiamin needed for the utilization of its carbohydrate, $\frac{1}{10}$ of the niacin required for the metabolism of the sugar, and about $\frac{1}{8}$ of the riboflavin.[2]

How to Prevent Iron Deficiency While Dieting

Anemia is a blood deficiency which, in general, is the result of the body not producing enough blood hemoglobin or enough red blood corpuscles.

The cause of anemia can be inadequate protein, iodine, ascorbic acid, B vitamins or a number of other factors. Many cases of anemia can be corrected by the addition of iron to the diet. In addition, foods with hydrochloric acid may be needed to free the iron for assimilation into the blood.

Foods which are high in iron and effective in the prevention or cure of anemia are Brewer's yeast, blackstrap molasses, wheat germ, liver, kidney, eggs, apricots and leafy vegetables. Foods that contain the acid needed to help with the absorption of iron are yogurt, buttermilk, oranges, lemons, and grapefruit.

One of the main reasons that even non-dieters incur anemia due to iron deficiency is the refining of sugar, flour and cereals. Blackstrap molasses is a by-product of the refining of sugar and one of the best sources of iron, containing about 10 milligrams per tablespoon as well as a number of other valuable minerals. The National Research Council recommends 12 milligrams of iron per day for adults, 15 milligrams for growing children.

There has been much talk about faddism in regard to such nutritive foods as yogurt and blackstrap molasses. However, these two especially are not any passing fancy. They have been used for centuries and have passed the test of time.

However, as long as they have not been adopted as part of their regular diet, people will attack special foods and those who eat them. I think it is worth a raised eyebrow or two to enjoy a raised level of bodily health, strength and energy. I urge my clients to investigate how to use blackstrap molasses, wheat germ, Brewer's

---

[2] "The Vitamins in Honey," *Journal of Nutrition*, Vol. 26, No. 3 (1943).

yeast and other powerful nutrients like them in their cooking and gourmet dining.

Where there is a will there is a way and when that way is found, the dividends in the enjoyment of life are immeasurable.

The World Is Your Supermarket

I have promised you a diet that is varied and delicious as well as slimming.

You may well be eating your way around the world as you dip into gourmet recipes by famous chefs everywhere. You will certainly have variety, probably more variety than you have been gaining weight on. Only now you will lose weight.

From China you may be dining on chicken or pork chow mein, barbequed ribs, and roast pork. From Italy there is minestrone soup, zucchini, and veal scallopini. France gives you bouillabaisse; Great Britain, finnan haddie; Russia, borscht. Or you can stay "domestic"—there are even foods to plan "New England" or "Western" style meals.

They have one thing in common. These are high-powered foods. They are bursting with vitality. They will improve the level of energy of anybody who has been growing fat on depleted carbo-hydrate—heavy foods.

A woman surprised me one day with the question, "Mr. Petrie, are you feeding me aphrodisiacs?"

"Why?"

"I feel so much more interested."

"Well," I countered, "don't you also feel more energetic and enthusiastic about other things as well?"

She had to admit that her increased "interest" reflected a higher level of total well-being.

I read somewhere recently that a health tonic was being pre-pared from the antlers of shy but lusty young deer by both New Zealand and Alaska. In New Zealand they call the product vita-deer and sell it as an essence that can be drunk directly to in-crease youthful zest. The Alaskans call their product a "secret love potion."

Antlers no, Brewer's yeast yes.

No, I offer you no aphrodisiacs, only powerful foods that offer more nutrients per calorie than any other diet you have probably ever seen.

Therein lies the miracle.

Miracle Step Six

Get to know the simple guidelines that help you to select one protein over another, but carve a big place for protein in your daily menu. Resolve to go easy on liquor and to detour around chemical additives in food. Taste some of the Miracle Diet foods that are new to you like blackstrap molasses, Brewer's yeast or yogurt. Experiment with new recipes that give your diet international horizons.

7

How to Use the Miracle Diet to Restore Youth

I have predicted that the Miracle Diet will make you look years younger.

It is no idle promise.

I, myself, have been thoroughly amazed when a client whom I have guessed to be in her late 40's comes in for her second visit a week later looking more like middle 30's.

I am *not* promising to take 15 years off your appearance in one week. But I am promising to move you in that youthful direction *fast*.

Mr. R. is a tall man. When he came to me he weighed 250 pounds. He appeared to be conscious of his height as he stooped slightly as if not to bump his head, although there was a two foot clearance between his six feet and my eight-foot ceiling. He seemed uncertain when he walked. His excessive weight and his poor posture made him look like he was pushing 60. Actually, he was only 44.

I soon found the cause of his overweight. He thoroughly enjoyed eating and drinking. The demands of his business required him to do both. His favorite drink was a Brandy Alexander (brandy, sweet cordial, and sweet cream). He would order one *or more* of these with his business lunches and in the evening when dining with clients.

I put him on the 1200-calorie, six-meal-a-day Miracle Diet. I watched his expression as I told him his type of drinking was out. He was ready to revolt. "I have to drink with my clients," he insisted, "or I'll be out of business." All right, I said, here's the only way you can drink. I then proceeded to interest him in the various vintages and types of champagne. He may have only dry (brut) champagne. He may experiment with various countries, vineyards, and production years. He can become an expert, if he wishes to impress his clients, but not one drop of anything else. I also showed him how to order fish and poultry in restaurants to get the most protein mileage for his caloric intake.

He cooperated.

In four months his weight was down to 170 pounds. He stood erect. His gait was decisive. He beamed when he told me the girls were looking at him again. He required less sleep and yet had more energy. "It must be those 1948 grapes," he said jokingly.

Whatever it was, he looked 35.

I have no bone to pick with the plastic surgeons that make you look "young" again. Every person owes it to himself or herself to look as youthful as possible. A face is lifted and the double chin is gone. Thighs are lifted and the flabby skin is gone. Arms are lifted and the tell-tale loose skin disappears. The buttocks are lifted and rounded.

However, I do feel uneasy about the ectomy—the blitzing of excess pounds under the surgeon's knife. It may be worth a few thousand dollars, painful convalescence and weeks in the hospital to get rid of 40 pounds of abdomen and thighs overnight. But I see the same person doing the same things, eating the same food and—you can guess the rest.

It takes a change to make a change.

Permanent change is the outcome of a decision to alter one's attitude or habits or both.

Can You Accept the Idea of Being Younger?

"How can I look younger?" you ask.

I could answer, "For one thing, instead of your regular brand of tea, drink Camomile. Its reputation for having powerful ingredients to prevent aging goes way back to the ancient Egyptians."

But I won't.

What chance of success can all the proteins, minerals, vitamins and herbs have if you are convinced you are old, getting older and wearing down under the burdens of the world?

It is not easy to change an attitude that has been with you a long time. Maybe for life. It is easier to change an eating habit than a thinking habit.

To change an eating habit, it takes a decision and the self-discipline to carry it out.

To change a thinking habit, it takes a decision, re-conditioning the mind through proper visualization, and the self-discipline to carry this out.

Can you accept the idea of being younger? Can you visualize yourself slender and youthful? Or do you believe you've had it? And that, in your case, there's no rolling back the clock.

I had a woman in her mid-thirties fail week after week on the Miracle Diet. There seemed to be any number of reasons why she could not make it work for her until one day she said to me, "I just can't see myself thin."

Then I knew the real reason for her failure. And I knew what to do.

I had a "before" picture of her in my file. I took the photo to a professional photographer friend of mine and I had him touch it up. He took pounds off her and removed signs of age—all via the touch-up brush.

When she arrived the following week with her tale of more woe, I reached for the picture and handed it to her.

She did not say a word, but as she looked at it, tears rolled down her cheeks.

It was what the psychologists call a "break-through."

From that moment on, she could see herself thin and younger. She liked what she saw. She kept the picture and looked at it often. And in a few short months she outdid the photographer.

Studies indicate that the process of aging can be slowed by eating smaller meals and eating more frequently.

Chalk one up for the Miracle Diet.

Other studies indicate that by limiting total daily food intake you can partially retard the process of aging.

Chalk one up again for the Miracle Diet.

Many studies indicate that overcoming nutritional deficiencies through the intake of sufficient protein, minerals and vitamins can restore vitality and a more youthful look.

Chalk still another one up for the Miracle Diet.

But suppose you have felt since childhood that you must have a full stomach in order to feel loved and secure. Or suppose as a man you have always felt that bigness is a symbol of stature, status and success. Or suppose your life so depressed you, your troubles so worried you, and your anxieties so burdened you, that you had grown to accept misery as "normal."

Wipe off all those chalk marks, because with those attitudes, all of the diets man can conceive are doomed to failure—even the Miracle Diet.

A famous pediatrician feels that the overweight problem starts with childhood and needs to be corrected in childhood. He believes that with adulthood, eating patterns are entrenched more firmly and reasons for dieting are rationalized away too easily. And he points out that 85 percent of all overweight children grow up to be overweight adults.

Besides putting them on 1200-calorie diets, the youngsters in this doctor's program get frequent counseling from physicians that help strengthen their resolve to lose weight.

If the reader is a youngster, fine. The path ahead will be that much easier. The adult will need more than just my counseling. The adult's path is more difficult in that there must be an undoing or neutralizing of perhaps years of negative visualizing that has shaped an attitude largely responsible for overweight and premature aging.

How to Think Thin and Young

Years of negative visualizing can be wiped out with minutes of positive visualizing.

The power of positive thinking has been vividly described by Dr. Norman Vincent Peale and even more vividly experienced by millions who have practiced what they have learned in his books.

I have taught thousands of men and women the art of visualizing positive images—seeing themselves eating the right food, growing slim and young, even dropping the smoking habit, getting rid of insomnia and fears, phobias and other unwanted habits.

Actually it is quite simple. Almost as easy as looking at a touched-up photo of yourself. Only you do it in your mind's eye.

Ideally speaking, it would help considerably if you were able to psychoanalyze yourself and determine just what attitudes were at the root cause of overeating. You might find out, for instance, that you needed love, or you were financially insecure. You could then add to your slender mental imaging, pictures of yourself surrounded and admired or pictures of yourself secure in the love and affection of family and friends.

Barring such an analysis, the slender images are powerful enough in themselves to re-condition your attitudes to accept a ten- to twenty-year younger *you*.

As a clinical hypnologist I have helped thousands of people to re-condition their subconscious mind in order to permit their body to accept new circumstances. Many thousands more have learned techniques to do this themselves in my book, *How to Reduce and Control Your Weight Through Self-Hypnotism*.[1] I have received letters from readers from as far away as Australia and South Africa and some written in French who read the French language edition.

I cannot condense that book into a few pages, so instead, I will give you the steps that need to be taken:

1. You relax thoroughly in a comfortable chair, so thoroughly that you feel on the verge of sleep.

---

[1] Prentice-Hall, Englewood Cliffs, New Jersey, 1965.

2. You quiet your mind so that it is free of miscellaneous thoughts. It helps to visualize grey or white clouds.

3. You visualize yourself as you know you can look—slender, vibrant, youthful and attractive.

This primes your subconscious to create what you visualize. It was so primed when you visualized that left-over pie in the refrigerator. Once you visualized that pie, chances are that your will was not powerful enough to resist the messages your subconscious machine gunned at you to go get it.

Imagination—the visual images you picture in your mind—always triumphs over willpower.

The purpose of the relaxation is to make those mental images sink in. If we are not thoroughly relaxed, and if our conscious mind is active and in control of the situation, then the images may not get through to the subconscious.

Imaging in a thoroughly relaxed state is like re-programming your mental computer to carry out your new orders.

One Minute a Day Can Take Years Off Your Appearance

The image that you see in a state of relaxation is the picture of the vigorous, youthful person you wish to be. You know that dropping poundage will help bring this about. You know that a diet of vital nutrients will help bring this about. So you visualize yourself nauseated by sickening sweet foods and fatty starches and you see yourself dining on foods that have the necessities of life built into them. You see yourself eating modestly—six times a day.

Let me help you with this visualizing. I will give you a monologue to follow. Not word for word, but once you have read it once or twice you can do it—mentally.

> I am sitting comfortably. . . . I let my arms drop limply by my sides. . . . I can feel their relaxed heaviness. . . . My whole body feels limp and heavy. . . . I breathe slowly and regularly as I do when asleep. . . . I get more deeply relaxed with each breath I take. . . . The heaviness creeps up my feet to legs, thighs and back. . . . My whole body feels

heavier and heavier. . . . I cannot keep my eyes open and they close gently. . . . My mind quiets in this relaxed state. . . . I no longer think thoughts. . . . I see a greyish white cloud from side to side and floor to ceiling. . . . I am quiet. . . . Now I see myself against the cloud. . . . I look slender and young, vibrant and energetic. . . . I know that as I arouse myself now I will be one step closer to that more perfect person. . . . I know I will feel re-charged and full of energy. . . . Now I open my eyes, move around in the chair, and I am wide awake.

Spend one minute a day in this enjoyable relaxation and I promise that you'll be winning a strong ally—your subconscious—over to your side in the battle of the bulge for the recapture of youth.

How to Reinforce the Mind's Role in Figure Control

You have made a fresh start. You are wiping out old eating habits and old attitudes and imbuing your mind and body with the vitality and energy of youth.

Builders of homes and other structures recognize milestones in their progress with suitable events. They hold ground-breaking ceremonies, topping-out parties (when they reach maximum building height) and finally dedication or cornerstone ceremonies.

Body builders can do well to make their progress milestones "official" too.

At this point in your fresh start, you need to perform just one act that proves to yourself a new page has been turned.

Do something different. Take a walk before breakfast. Go to work by a different route. Telephone somebody you haven't spoken to in a long while. Clean a closet or straighten a drawer. Buy a new bauble. Put on a new tie.

Take a sauna or a steam bath or a massage.

If you are creative, paint a picture, sew, sculpt, knit or write.

Break out of the old pattern. Go to the zoo. Try anything new.

Believe it or not this act of symbolizing a "new start" has a powerful effect. It is exhilarating. It clears the mental air, so to speak, and prepares the psychological climate for change. Indeed, it gives that change dramatic momentum.

A man I knew had a weakness for snacking at every hot dog stand, luncheonette, or pizzeria he passed. When he started the Miracle Diet and prepared his psychological climate with mental relaxation, he "made it official" by taking a walk to his favorite snack joints and walking up and down in front of them several times to prove he no longer had to go in.

Noted psychologist Joyce Brothers recommends some non-stomach-oriented self-indulgence. Buying that proverbial new hat or pair of shoes can be a tonic, she says, and you can back it up by taping a "before" picture of yourself at your heaviest on the refrigerator door.

Whether you play a game like "fatty on the icebox" or merely take a walk around the block you are converting intention into action. You have made your decision official.

You have proved that you are ready to accept that slender, youthful version of yourself.

Diet Can Prolong Human Life

In India, the Hunzas live decades longer than man's average life span. Centenarians are quite common. They are a cheerful people and capable of great physical endurance without a sign of fatigue.

Physicians and others who have studied the Hunza environment in the Himalayas have been impressed with the richness of the soil. Although their variety of foods is limited, they are grown in a soil that is naturally fertilized and watered by mountain streams rich in minerals.

The Hunzas are not alone. Scientists have made similar studies of primitive peoples in South America, Mexico, and Africa, where sickness is rare and longevity prevails. One factor is always present: natural foods rich in nutrients.

Yes, diet can keep us young longer. There is no doubt of that. In fact, scientists are working on this fact of life to extend life beyond anything now thought possible.

Medical News, published in London, recently carried a story about experiments with mice where they have been kept alive way beyond their normal life span by feeding them substances that counteract "free radicals." These are electrons turned loose in the body by the breaking of bonds between atoms in enzyme and other biological reactions. Free radicals are believed to cause deleterious aging changes in living organisms.

Aging occurs as protein-starved cells die out. This is not necessarily due to a protein shortage. Cells have a protein cycle. For the first 20 years protein in human cells builds up. For the next 20 years, from age 20 to 40, there is a protein balance. After 40, there is a tendency for cell protein to break down. We need more protein in later years to slow aging.

This aging cycle can be *accelerated:* by a hard life—mentally and physically—coupled with nutritional deficiences, especially of protein.

The aging cycle can also be *slowed:* by body care and, of course, nutritional efficiency.

Scientists say that the weight of a 75-year-old man's brain is less than that of a 30-year-old man due to cell loss. They are hot on the trail of answering the question of why these cells die, thanks to biochemistry's ability now to identify the structure of the DNA molecule (deoxyribonucleic acid). This is the key portion of a cell's nucleus.

Although they do not yet know just how, they strongly suspect that it is the DNA molecule that affects life, aging and death.

And I strongly suspect that the proteins we eat and the positive thoughts we think beneficially affect the DNA molecule.

How to Enjoy a Radiant, Youthful Skin

The worn, jaded look of aging is supplied largely by the skin. The skin is quick to reveal unwholesome eating or unwholesome thoughts. Since the "look" of youth or middle years or old age is actually the appearance of the skin, we should care for our skin and treat it as we would a vital organ such as our heart.

Skin is protein. A healthy, glowing skin requires a diet abundant in protein. Dermatologists say that certain vitamins are important to skin health: B_1 (thiamine), B_2 (riboflavin), and B_6 (pyridoxine). This is one of the reasons I have mentioned Brewer's yeast. It is an excellent source of these B vitamins.

Skin tone also depends on good blood circulation. Foods that contribute to a healthy blood circulation are those that contain such minerals as iron, calcium and iodine and vitamins A, B, and C.

Unsaturated fatty acids contribute to a glowing, youthful skin. Such salad oils as corn oil, wheat germ oil, safflower oil or olive oil are a good skin tonic when at least a tablespoon is consumed each day. Psoriasis and eczema conditions improve with this treatment. Corn oil, which contains linoleic acid, is especially effective for eczema.

You can feed your skin from the outside, too. A beauty mask of raw egg white has long been popular with exclusive salons. The skin absorbs it readily and it acts as an instant tonic for tired skin cells.

The skin also needs minerals and vitamins. A peaches and cream complexion was actually named for its use on the skin. When grandmother was young, today's manufactured cosmetics did not exist and she used mixtures such as peaches and cream blended into a lotion. Sometimes she mixed in strawberries, sometimes cucumbers, experimenting with the results which were often quite dramatic.

Dryness is a common skin problem. Natural oils can be restored through applications of coconut oil, castor oil, olive oil or lanolin. Almond oil and honey is a favorite skin lotion that goes back centuries in use.

Wrinkles? Away with them. Rub castor oil into wrinkled facial areas. For wrinkles under the skin apply moist tea bags for a few minutes daily.

Poisons to the skin are products that contain sugar. Sugar is the chief culprit behind skin blemishes. Other poisons are contained in deodorants and cosmetics. The chemicals and detergents in them can cause serious irritation.

Fortunately, your skin thrives on the same Miracle Diet ingredients that you thrive on—proteins, vitamins and minerals in their natural state.

Coffee and Tea—Are They Beneficial Beverages?

There are six meals a day on The Miracle Diet. For breakfast No. 1, lunch No. 1 and dinner No. 1 I have scheduled a choice of coffee or tea. Neither is itemized on the No. 2 meals.

There is the admonition that coffee shall be black, and tea with only lemon.

Although coffee and tea of themselves are virtually calorie-less, the entourage of calories that can accompany them in the form of sugar, cream and side dishes can be a threat to any diet.

They are important to the morale. They make a meal "complete" because we have grown accustomed to a hot beverage as the "finis." So I am willing to take a calculated risk and say OK three times a day.

Why three times and not six? There is caffeine in coffee and tea. Caffeine is an ingredient that is non gratis for persons with heart trouble, arthritis, high blood pressure, ulcers and liver disease. Even without these health problems, caffeine can produce others. Moderation is in order.

Every time you drink a cup of coffee or tea, you trigger the liver to produce blood sugar (you feel a lift because of this). This, in turn, triggers the pancreas to secrete insulin. Result: An extra work load for these two vital organs.

Coffee and tea do have nutritional pluses on their side. They are not all bad. Coffee is rich in niacin, one of the B vitamins. But then again there are those who argue that caffeine, by stimulating the heartbeat, causes B vitamins to be lost in the urine, causing a shortage of B vitamins among heavy coffee drinkers.

Tea soaks minerals out of dried tea leaves and its nutritive value depends on the kind of tea. If in doubt, swing to the herb teas that are healthful beyond question:

- Rose hip tea contains large quantities of Vitamin C and helps prevent colds.
- Sassafras tea has been used for centuries to help rheumatism and skin complaints.
- Papaya tea helps digestion.

- Peppermint tea helps digestion, too, and is an old stand-by remedy for headaches and nervousness.
- Fenugreek tea is rich in lecithin, phosphates, iron and choline. It is a fever antidote as well as an aid to good nutrition. Some call it an aphrodisiac.
- Alfalfa tea is rich in valuable minerals because its roots grow deep in the soil. It is also a source of vitamins A, D, E and G and is useful in relieving arthritic pains.

Again I warn against sugar. If you must have sugar in coffee or tea, I say do without the beverage. You are better off drinking water.

Another hazard to drinking coffee these days is the new non-dairy "creamers" that are being used more and more widely. I would favor the calories of whole milk or cream over the following chemicals which I copied from the label on one such artificial product:

> sorbitol
> sodium caseinate
> glycerol
> sugar
> emulsifiers
> di-potassium phosphate
> salt
> artificial flavor
> artificial color

The Value of Food Supplements

How would you like a diet of caribou, seal, white whale and polar bear balanced off in the summer time with some sorrel and arctic willow plants dipped in seal oil. A study of Eskimos sponsored some 15 years ago in Norway disclosed that the basal metabolism of Eskimos in their native habitat living on their own native diet was significantly higher than whites. When given the white man's diet this basal metabolism rate was reduced to the level of whites.

Eskimos have tremendous powers of endurance. They are seldom overweight. Tooth decay, arthritis, cancer and other degenerative diseases are rare.

One thing about caribou, as opposed to cattle, it grazes on wild plants that live in natural undepleted soil and which are therefore rich in nutrients.

Europeans and Asians, who have understood over the centuries that farmers must return nutrients to the soil, have composted their soil with leaves, manure and other organic material. This is difficult, if not impossible, to do on the large commercial scale of American farming.

When they dine for the first time in this country, Europeans notice a lack of taste in American vegetables. Nutritionists who compare vegetables grown on composted versus non-composted soil have come up with figures approaching twice as much nutrients in the composted grown crops.

Furthermore, the commercial processing of food, albeit economically necessary to prevent financial loss due to spoilage in transit and to improve looks and packability, takes another swipe at natural nutrients.

Before it reaches us, our food is "anemic" due to under-nourished soil. Much is harvested unripe because of the time lag between farm and table, and is therefore still further below nutritional par. And as if that is not enough, it is sprayed, refined, bleached, preserved, boiled, colored, adulterated and doctored. Even then, after it arrives in our kitchen, storage and cooking further depletes what we eventually put in our mouth.

Should the word "fortified" on the label give you heart, just remember that what is put back into bread and other processed foods is usually less than one third of what has been removed.

So what do we do about it?

The person who seeks fresh, local nutritious foods may succeed on the fresh and the local, but still not be getting the required nutrients.

It is this dilemma that has led to the rapid growth of the vitamin and food supplement industry.

I find myself in a bind. I advocate the fresh and the natural, yet I still find I must occasionally recommend capsules and powders.

Vitamins and other supplements have become a necessity of American life. I believe that most people, desirous of peak health through complete nutrition, must inevitably be led to some such reinforcement.

We are a busy people. We must eat what is available and what takes little time to prepare. It is better to correct than to ignore the inevitable deficiencies.

Food Supplements

I favor the following basic supplements:

LECITHIN

This is a component of the nervous system. We deplete our body's supply of it as we work under stress. Supplements are obtained largely from soybeans and can be taken by sprinkling on food. About 17 percent of the brain is lecithin. It helps the body use Vitamins A, D, and E, and it helps prevent accumulations of cholesterol by keeping it emulsified. I place it at the top of the list because lecithin is a recognized boon to cell regeneration and as such can prolong youth and lengthen life.

VITAMINS

A, B, C, D and E. Look for fish-liver oil vitamins capsules for the A and D, dried liver and other dried organ meats for the B complex vitamins, and rose hips for C.

KELP

This, coming from the sea, abounds with amino acids, vitamins and minerals. It is more commonly known as seaweed. Although the body needs just a trace of iodine to maintain a balanced metabolism this minute quantity is hard to come by in other foods. It is abundant in kelp.

These items are in health food stores and are also available by mail from a number of suppliers throughout the country. Your physician can give you further information about quantities and benefits.

You Can Postpone Old Age for Decades

Medical research is devising new weapons for use in the battle against such illnesses of old age as arthritis, heart trouble, kidney ailments, nervous disorders, respiratory difficulties, etc. However, geriatric research, by looking at the whole person, not just the heart by itself, the lungs or the kidneys, is on the threshold of great accomplishments.

As the body grows older, it can no longer handle the "loads" we put on it. Yet we give it the same amount of the daily stress of modern living. And we give it the same amount of food to digest, metabolize or store.

An overtaxed organ degenerates faster and can even suffer acute failure. We must ease up the load on our body's organs as we advance in years *before* these degenerations and failures, not as a result of them. According to geriatric research, this means:

1. Continued mild exercise, but less physical exertion
2. A balanced diet, but fewer total calories
3. No large meals, but rather more frequent small meals

Exercise like walking, swimming and gardening help keep the organs toned up. You can feel invigorated after this type of mild, healthful exercise rather than exhausted, fatigued or depleted. Oh, you're tired, but it's a good feeling with an aura of healthful accomplishment behind it.

A balanced diet with all the proteins, minerals and vitamins is even more important for older people. There is just one difficulty. As I mentioned earlier, the body's assimilation of proteins slows up after 40. Proteins are still needed, but the body cannot handle as much protein as it used to.

As a result, older people can develop kidney trouble or other malfunctions from too much protein.

However, they still need the amino acids in protein. So they must emphasize those protein foods in which these amino acids are all present in balanced, easy to assimilate proportions. Geriatric research points to liver, lean beef, fish and poultry.

Well, fine. The Miracle Diet has been postponing old age on this score. It, too, has been emphasizing these proteins.

Geriatric research divides carbohydrates into good carbohydrates and bad carbohydrates. Good carbohydrates are the whole grains, fresh fruits and green non-starchy vegetables. The bad carbohydrates? You guessed it—candy, cake, and other sugary, starchy "foods." Score another point for the Miracle Diet.

I was listening to a radio program one morning called the University Explorer, sponsored by the University of California. Dr. Josef P. Hrachovec, a geriatric researcher who believes we can live to 100 or longer, was being quoted on the subject of three meals a day. Man used to be a nibbler, he had said, a creature accustomed to small, frequent feedings. This is still his natural way. But the routines of civilized life require him to eat a hurried breakfast, if any at all, a light lunch, and a big body-straining dinner. Dr. Hrachovec recommended smaller, more frequent meals starting with a modest, nutritious breakfast.

Score another point for the Miracle Diet. While it slenderizes and rejuvenates, it is also postponing the spectre of degeneration and debilitation.

I think it is very heartening that the younger generation is more nutrition-minded than ever before. The so-called hippies and flower-children "feel" the need for natural foods grown in replenished soil.

It may be part of the generation gap, but a good part, that young people are taking a new look at old ways and coming up with wheat germ, soybean flour, and yogurt.

The children of today are the parents of tomorrow. Hopefully, their eating habits will carry mankind a step away from artificial, time-saving concoctions and a step closer to natural, nutritional foods.

Miracle Step Seven

Analyze your attitude toward yourself. Do you really invite a slender figure and can you accept a more youthful look? Practice reconditioning your mind to think thin and young. Strive for deeper relaxation, more vivid visualization each time. Spend a minute a day at it. Understand how diet can restore youth. Try feeding your skin and hair protein to see the difference this can make. Consider making changes away from some beverages to others that are more nutritious. Select some high potency food supplement to accelerate the changes that are about to occur.

8

How to Use the Miracle Diet for Attractiveness and Sexual Fulfillment

Whether we know it or not, or whether we are willing to admit it to ourselves: a sense of buoyant well-being is largely an interest in the opposite sex.

Men cannot boast youthfulness and health unless they can also boast virility and vigor.

Women cannot boast youthfulness and health unless they can also boast feminine attractiveness and desire for sexual fulfillment.

There are two ways to attain this:

1. You can use aphrodisiacs—special foods that titillate the sex glands and organs and stimulate sexual activity.
2. You can nourish the entire body including the glands so that all organs function at a high metabolic level, thus stimulating sexual activity.

I prefer the second method.

There are reference books on aphrodisiacs and those who prefer this localized approach to vigor can find what they need to know.

How Six Meals a Day Increases Sexual Potency

In 1935, two Yale faculty members made a study[1] of the effects of frequency of meals on physical efficiency. They found that more frequent feedings reduced fatigue, irritability and muscular inefficiency. Now they may not have been referring to sexual performance, but I pity the one whose sexual partner is beset by any one of those three.

Since this book you are now reading waves three major banners:

1. Six calorie-controlled meals a day
2. Adequate protein
3. Abundance of other nutrients

I am going to tell you how the reverse side of these banners proclaim "Sexual Pleasure."

Why in the world would six modest meals make a person more sexually interesting and interested?

It's a long, complicated chemical story, but I'm going to oversimplify it just to get the main concept across quickly to you. Follow along.

Proteins are not just proteins. They are made up of about 22 different substances called amino acids in thousands of combinations. Meat, fish, eggs, cheese, soy beans, though up to 100 percent protein, have different combinations of amino acids and may be totally devoid of some.

Since the body needs all of these amino acids for different cell-construction jobs, *the more that are present in the digestive system at one time* the better we satisfy our total bodily needs.

Six meals a day—as opposed to three—increases the chances that a complete spectrum of amino acids is present at one time.

As I said before, this is an over-simplification, but it points to one more causative factor behind the miracle in the Miracle Diet.

---

[1] Howard W. Haggard, M.D. and Leon A. Greenberg, Ph.D., "Diet and Physical Efficiency—The Influence of Frequency of Meals upon Physical Efficiency and Industrial Productivity" (New Haven, Conn.: Yale University Press).

It follows that if the sex glands, called gonads, need an important protein to operate at top potential and one amino acid is not available, you might want to read a good book instead.

For instance, if amino acids A and B are available in the morning, but amino acid C, which A and B require to complete the gonad protein, is not available at that time, no gonad protein. Sex relations can be good, but not the best.

Should amino acid C enter the intestinal picture that evening, thanks say to broiled calf's liver on dinner no. 1, amino acids A and B may have already been assimilated for a different protein on the body's "priority call list."

The sex glands must then wait until amino acids A, B and C are all present at the same time.

The odds for this happening on six nutritious meals a day are at least twice as good as on three.

A specific example: it is now suspected that a deficiency of argenine, previously thought to be a non-essential amino acid, can markedly effect the production of male sperm.

All of which brings us back to proteins.

Protein Affects Sexual Desire

The breakdown of the protein-starved body is pitiful to see. The pictures of African children with pot bellies and skinny frames are the classic ones that come to mind.

But one does not have to travel very far to find that typical protein-starved person. The man with the rounded shoulders, protruding stomach, bowed head, flabby skin and apathetic look. Or consider a woman with not a curve on her body, dull complexion, aimless gait.

A six-meal high protein diet promotes an active sexual life three ways:

1. A person free of excess weight due to a carbohydrate-heavy diet is a healthier, more vigorous person.
2. A person free of protein deficiencies due to a high protein diet is able to perform all of life's functions more effectively.
3. A person who distributes protein over six meals instead of three improves total glandular nutrition.

Furthermore, protein deficiency is highly suspect in unsatisfactory reproduction: difficulties in conception, spontaneous abortions, and infant deformities.

The Tiny Gland That Says Yes or No to Sex

Hormones, the regulator of our life functions, are produced by our endocrine glands.

Most of these endocrine glands, recent research tells us, are dependent in various degrees on the functioning of the "master" gland known as the pituitary.

This tiny gland is located at the base of the brain. It manufactures at least 12 different hormones, all vital to a high level of health.

No bigger than the size of a pea, the pituitary gland is like the president's office in a multi-million dollar corporation. Here are where the decisions are made and the orders go out.

It is instrumental in the maintenance, repair and growth of the factory itself because it directs and controls the growth of bones and tissues. It stimulates the sex glands and directs the activities of the ovaries. It is in control of the insulin-producing pancreas. It is the indirect controller of the appetite and of sleep through its effect on the nearby hypothalamus gland. It contributes hormones needed for the healthy functioning of the brain and nervous system.

It is obvious that a healthy pituitary is essential for a vigorous sex tone and prolonged youthfulness. Your contribution to its health can be in the form of

- Diversified proteins daily
- In a continuous six-meal supply
- Backed up by a general mineral and vitamin supplement
- Further strengthened by a B-complex supplement.

The Gland That Acts as Sexual Brake or Accelerator

Another gland that plays an important sexual role in the process of carrying out its total vital function is the thyroid. Located in the neck, this gland determines the speed at which you live.

A metabolic rate is set by the thyroid. A fast rate can keep you in a state of nervous activity, a slow rate in a state of listless doldrums.

The key is iodine. The thyroid gland needs iodine to produce thyroxin, the hormone that controls growth among other things.

Actually only minute quantities of iodine are needed. But they are vital to life itself. People who seldom eat fish and who don't use garlic are missing the two best sources of iodine. Sea salt is rich in iodine, but not after it has been purified for our dining room table.

You can supplement your iodine, if ocean fish is not available or to your liking, by buying iodized salt always on health food store shelves or by adding kelp (dried seaweed), also found at health food stores, to soups and other recipes.

Iodine and iron get together in the body and work sex magic. Sexual potency makes giant strides. The blood vessels, heart, brain and endocrine system go along for the health ride. In women, the two ingredients are expended more than in men, because of the processes of menstruation, gestation and lactation.

Mrs. M. weighed 20 pounds too much. Since she was only 5 feet two inches, it showed, and she knew it. When she came to me, she appeared to be very nervous and confessed she had not dated since her recent divorce.

I asked her why she was so "jumpy." "I don't know," she said, "I feel it might be the cut-throat competition among us salesladies at the department store where I work, but I can't prove it."

A few more minutes of conversation with her and I began to sense there was more to it than competition. She had a low opinion of herself and was worry prone. Her chief worry was beneath the surface: Would she retain her sexual appeal and be able to attract men again?

Mrs. M. went on the 1200-calorie six-meal-a-day Miracle Diet. She enjoyed fish and greens and we emphasized these. She consulted her physician about diet supplements and he recommended combination vitamin capsules.

In a month and a half she had lost nine pounds. Her self-confidence improved. She was less sensitive about what people said. She seemed more poised and less jittery. Last I saw of Mrs. M. she was within five pounds of normal. She was modeling dresses in the department store. And she was dating again.

An improperly functioning thyroid gland can cause sex glands to become lazy. An overactive thyroid gland can cause an individual to almost "burn himself out." When a thyroid gland is not adequately nourished, it can begin to wane. In senile people, the thyroid gland is invariably atrophied.

Seeds and Sex

In many parts of the world, the favorite snack is seeds. In Mexico it's pumpkin seeds. In Russia it's sunflower seeds. In the Middle East it's sesame seeds.

People are "cagey" about offering any reason behind the popularity of seeds. "I like them" is the usual retort. More frankness might produce, "I like them because they take the edge off my food appetite and put the edge on my other appetites."

There's more of a connection between seeds and sex than the fact that they contain the germ of life.

They also contain lecithin.

I recommend seeds for a snack. I recommend lecithin as a food supplement. If I need to convince you that they heighten sexual virility and pleasure in order to motivate you to eat them—all right, they do.

Every cell in our body contains lecithin. A major deficiency can lead to sexual impotence. A slight deficiency can lead to irritability and a feeling of exhaustion.

"Not tonight, dear, I have a headache."

Seeds are actually a complete food. While they are upping our sexual energy, they are nourishing the whole body. They are 50 percent high quality protein, some unsaturated fats, and the rest carbohydrate. They contain as much, if not more, lecithin than soybeans. They are rich sources of the B-vitamins and minerals.

Thanks to our knowledge of nutrition, seeds are no longer strictly for the birds.

How Vitamins Affect Sexual Activity

Since the early 1900s, some 50 vitamins have been isolated. Of these, 25 have been proved to be essential to the proper functioning of our body—and that means essential to life itself.

This does not mean that the other score or more of identified vitamins are useless to the body. It merely means that we are still in the dark about their function—if any.

The body cannot manufacture vitamins. It can absorb them, assimilate them or excrete them.

But you must provide them.

Do you know any of these people?—

Arthur is being seen with other (much younger) women. His wife has asked for a separation.

Myrtle is pregnant again after two miscarriages. Will she be able to go all the way this time?

What will happen to Bill's job as a film editor now that he's having all that trouble with his eyes.

Pamela is in hiding again. What an attractive girl she'd be if it weren't for that skin!

They are very likely the vitamins-minus people. They blame it all on the other woman, on a virus, or on plain bad luck.

They just don't know their A, B, C's of Vitamins.

VITAMIN A

Experiments on animals show that deficiencies of this vitamin lead to poor fertilization, abnormal embryonic growth, placental injury, and occasional death of the fetus. Large doses of Vitamin A prolonged life 10 percent. In humans, deficiencies cause impairment of bone formation, digestive system, respiratory tract, skin, and genitals. It is an essential factor in the vigorous functioning of the sex glands, particularly the testes. It insures vitality in new cell growth, resistance to infections, delay in senility and increased longevity.

SOURCES: Dandelion greens, turnip greens, collards, squash, broccoli, mustard greens, kale, calf's liver.

VITAMIN B₁

When in short supply, a diminishing of hormones and a lessening of sexual desire results. There is a loss of appetite and muscular tone. Noticeable symptoms could be distended abdomen, dry hair, fatigue, irritability or constipation. Known as thiamine, its dietary abundance is a tonic to digestion, muscle tone, and sexual relations.

SOURCES: Brewer's yeast, soybeans, wheat germ, brown rice, seeds, beef heart, beef kidney, oysters, eggs, some pork cuts. It is soluble in water and easily destroyed by heat so source foods that are cooked are not as valuable as yeast, wheat germ, seeds and oysters.

VITAMIN B₂

Known as riboflavin, its lack affects the eyes leading to itching, burning, watering and a bloodshot condition. Lack can also cause nervous depression, loss of hair, dermatitis, diminished vitality including lessened sexual potential. In adequate amounts it is beneficial to the hair, skin, eyes, and soft tissues of the body including muscles. It clears brown blemishes on the skin, improves cellular exchange of oxygen, and is said to increase resistance to fungus diseases like athlete's foot.

SOURCES: The same vegetable sources as Vitamin A plus skimmed milk, organ meats, Brewer's yeast and wheat germ.

VITAMIN B₆

This is pyridoxine. Without it there is tendency to tooth decay, poor muscle tone. Still being investigated, its absence in canine diets has caused arteriosclerosis. In our diet it has a definite sedative effect. It improves muscle tone and is used in the treatment of muscular dystrophy, multiple sclerosis, and other nerve-muscle disorders.

SOURCES: Find it in bran and whole wheat cereals, most meats, especially liver, and in fresh leafy vegetables.

VITAMIN B₁₂

This is the animal protein factor essential for the blood-forming function of bone marrow because it alone contains cobalt. It is especially important to the central nervous system upon which the enjoyment of sexual relations depends. Critical during pregnancy. It stimulates growth in retarded children, helps to combat pernicious anemia and slows degeneration of the nerves.

SOURCES: Not found in vegetables, only in liver, meat and milk.

VITAMIN B

Nicotinic acid, otherwise known as niacin, is one more B vitamin so important to the complex operations of the brain and nervous system. Its shortage can lead to nerve disorders ranging from neurasthenia to insanity. In abundance it contributes to hair growth and hair health by increasing blood circulation to hair follicles. Helpful in certain cases of migraine. Needed for normal healthy liver function.

SOURCES: Look to liver, lean meats, fish, poultry, yeast and bran.

OTHER B VITAMINS

Also in the B-complex family are Pantothenic acid, Folic acid, Choline, Para-amenobenzoic acid (PABA), Biotin, Inositol and others. Generally speaking they are needed for interaction with other vitamins. Little is known about some of them. Folic acid aids the effects of female hormones. Its presence in fenugreek seeds, together with choline and lecithin, undoubtedly contributes to their alleged sex-provoking attribute. PABA aids glandular function and, together with Vitamin E (see below), is reported to have a distinct aphrodisiac effect. It has been used favorably in the treatment of sterility in women. Recent research has shown that B-complex vitamins affect the production of sperm, ovum, the mating urge, and the entire sexual cycle, including maternal instinct, embryonic development and lactation.

SOURCES: All of the above food sources.

VITAMIN C

Ascorbic acid is fundamental in the production of collagen, a protein used by the body in the formation of skin, tendons, and bone as well as supportive and connective tissue. Frequently referred to as the glue that holds the cells of the body together, chalk it up as essential to milady's mammary development as well as her well-turned calf, attractive legs, and curvaceous thighs. Without it—varicose veins, gum trouble, possible eye cataracts, and just plain "sag." The adrenal glands need ascorbic acid to stimulate them in the production of cortin, a hormone highly instrumental in fighting disease and infection. Smokers are quite likely to be deficient in Vitamin C because one cigarette is said to destroy 25 mg. of Vitamin C in the body as compared to 60 mg. which is the minimum adult daily requirement. Some nutritionists recommend as much as 1200 mg. daily. These large doses markedly increase resistance to colds.

SOURCES: Fresh citrus fruits, strawberries, watermelon, cantaloupe, tomatoes, cabbage, brussels sprouts, peppers, broccoli, cauliflower, rose hips. Cooking in water destroys much of the Vitamin C content as does long exposure to air.

VITAMIN D

Without this vitamin, the body cannot absorb calcium readily from foods. Result: poor bone structure and teeth. Exposure to the sun permits the body to manufacture its own Vitamin D. It is helpful in treating acne and arthritis. Overdosages can be dangerous leading to all the symptoms of sun poisoning or sunstroke. Another benefit—indirectly it promotes the body's use of phosphorus also essential to bone structure.

SOURCES: Few foods contain significant amounts. The synthetic Vitamin D is said to be dangerous to the kidneys. Fish liver oil supplements are fine. Modest amounts are in sunflower seeds (aptly named), butter, eggs and milk.

VITAMIN E

Essential to the normal functioning of the cardiovascular system. Often called the sex vitamin, it is important in the condition of the reproductive glands and the maintenance of sexual potency. Vitamin E deficiency in animals results in testicular degeneration and sterility. Impotency in men and frigidity in women respond well to diets rich in Vitamin E,

A, thiamine, iron, and, of course, protein. It offers relief for women in menopause by controlling such unpleasant symptoms as hot flashes, backache, and excessive menstrual flow. Along with A, Vitamin E guards against liver disturbances, persistent headaches, dry skin. It aids hair health and skin beauty.

SOURCES: Get it from corn oil, soy oil, wheat germ oil, cottonseed oil, whole grains, corn, spinach, most leafy vegetables, meat, eggs and seeds.

VITAMIN F

This is the unsaturated fatty acid. It helps the body absorb most other vitamins, distributes calcium, contributes to growth and general good health. Without it there can be a tendency to arteriosclerosis. With it, there is resistance to disease, proper maintenance of cholesterol level and body warmth (not connected necessarily with sexual temperature). A beauty aid for hair, skin and nails.

SOURCES: Grain and vegetable oils, seed fats, particularly wheat germ, safflower, peanut, soybean and sunflower oils. Daily use in salads and cooking would supply sufficient quantities.

VITAMIN K

Japanese scientists have recently made claims that Vitamin K is an important agent in human longevity. Its cardinal role is the formation of prothrombin in the liver, essential for the clotting of blood. A lack causes persistent hemorrhaging. It has been used successfully as part of the treatment of coronary thrombosis. Sex applications? Remote, unless you live and love longer.

SOURCES: All green, leafy vegetables, tomatoes, alfalfa, egg yolk, soybean oil, liver.

VITAMIN P

These bioflavonoids are composed of rutin, citrin and hesperidin. Acting in consort with other vitamins and minerals, they keep blood vessel walls in healthy condition, especially the tiny veins and capillaries. Don't overlook the fact that these are essential in sexual arousal of erogenous zones, but, of course, their overall bodily functions enhance cell feeding and cellular waste removal. Excellent protection against many malfunctions and diseases. Truly a miracle substance, it is found in many Miracle Diet foods.

SOURCES: Spinach, parsley, green peppers, citrus fruits, lettuce, watercress, cabbage, carrots, apples.

Minerals and Sex Power

Whenever people think of mineral-poor blood they think of a commercial product ("with all that iron") because of the extensive national advertising of that product.

It is no coincidence that middle-aged show biz folk appear in such commercials and one comes away with a feeling that they use the supplement to prolong their exciting lives.

No doubt about the enervating aspect to iron-poor blood.

We lose iron through perspiration, nail and hair cuttings, elimination, and—in women—menstruation. We need to restore iron and other minerals to our bodies in order to assume a sound structure and health functioning. They help build bone, teeth, nails, hair and muscle. They are needed in the control of acidity and alkalinity which is a sensitive factor in total body chemistry, and they act as catalysts in many vital chemical reactions.

With general mineral deficiencies, all of the body functions would suffer. Nerve message sending would be impaired, water levels so necessary to life processes would be thrown off balance, and many nutrients could not be assimilated by the body.

The key minerals are:

Calcium
Iron
Phosphorus
Copper
Manganese
Iodine
Potassium
Sodium

CALCIUM

Well known as the builder of teeth, bones and nails, calcium's use by the body is regulated by the two parathyroid glands. It is the most abundant mineral in the body and therefore a key mineral in any diet and in any bodily function, including such a basic one as sexual activity. Young or old, we always need calcium. Without it the disorders that result affect every part of the body. Lack of calcium can result even if it is plentiful in the food we eat because some foods and drugs block its absorption. Suspect are white bread, chocolate, and DDT.

SOURCES: Milk, most cheeses, blackstrap molasses, egg yolk, olives, green vegetables, seafood, poultry, whole grains.

IRON

So much has been said so far about iron, let me just sum up by emphasizing that it enables the blood to carry essential oxygen throughout the body and helps remove carbon dioxide from body cells. Contributes to quick thinking and mental alertness.

SOURCES: You guessed right. Leafy greens, liver, soybeans, wheat germ. Also egg yolk, blackstrap molasses, bran.

PHOSPHORUS

Works like calcium and in conjunction with it. Sustains fluid content of the brain. Reinforces nerves and muscles. Essential to glandular secretions and muscle contraction, sex fans. Actually it is an essential element in every body tissue.

SOURCES: Most protein foods have phosphorus—meats, fish, cheese, eggs, poultry. And would you believe soybeans and whole wheat?

COPPER

Anemia is the price of copper deficiency because it works hand in glove with iron. It also lends the body a hand in the use of Vitamin C. Grey hair can be a sign of copper shortage as the metal plays a part in pigment formation.

SOURCES: Usually found in the same foods as iron. For some reason it is abundant in huckleberries and oatmeal!

MANGANESE

Can cause a loss of interest in the sexual act. Absence interferes with the maternal instinct and normal reproductive functions. It activates a number of enzymes and works together with calcium phosphorus. It is practically eliminated from refined food products.

SOURCES: Find it in whole grains and cereals, green vegetables if not grown in depleted soil.

IODINE

We have discussed how this is essential to the functioning of the thyroid gland, regulator of the body's metabolic rate. Improperly regulated, it can produce a sluggish person with no interest in life, much less sex. Normal thyroid functioning produces stamina and vitality for work or play.

SOURCES: Ocean fish, shellfish, iodized salt.

POTASSIUM

Lost when soil is depleted or in vegetable cooking water, potassium is nerve food, heart food, and muscle food. When under-supplied we suffer constipation, indigestion, insomnia, irritability—not exactly the climate for a love nest.

SOURCES: Green leafy vegetables, kelp, cranberries, tomatoes, apple cider vinegar, blackstrap molasses, carrots, cucumbers, honey, many fruits.

SODIUM

Aids in the absorption of all of the above minerals into the blood. Enough said?

SOURCES: In normally salted foods.

A Word of Advice to the Love-Lorn

The Miracle Diet is designed to keep your body thoroughly nourished and operating at peak efficiency while you lose weight. If you are the average overweight person, you will notice a marked boost in your level of health, sexual interest, energy, and vitality as soon as you begin it.

After a number of weeks on it, you will feel like a new person. Your friends will notice the difference.

There is no need to take a daily inventory of each vitamin and each mineral. Such a boxscore is a waste of time. Spend the time instead on assuring yourself of the right foods six times a day. When in doubt add food supplements previously discussed.

Miracle Step Eight

Make the improvement of sexual activity a result of a general heightening in total bodily well-being. Associate six meals a day, vitamin-rich and mineral-packed foods as part of your program for a fuller sex life. By understanding the glands involved and how each vitamin and mineral affects your body you can select those foods or food supplements that hold greatest promise for you.

$$9$$

Special Miracle Diets
for Special Uses

Are you somebody special?

Do you take your meals on the run?

Or are you on a restricted diet due to an illness?

Possibly you are a vegetarian? Or some other kind of an "—arian."

The average person just does not exist. We all have special factors in our life that shape our activities. We all have more time or less time—more chance or less chance—more facility or less facility.

Many of us have health problems that we have learned to live with. Others have family problems. Or career problems.

Mrs. T. was 35. She had been underweight all of her life. To remedy this, she went on a vitamin binge and created such a hunger that she soon ate her way up from 103 pounds to 196 pounds!

When she came to me she considered herself pleasingly plump (she was five feet six inches tall) but her husband did not appreciate her new look. He felt that the ninety pounds of extra wife had settled in the wrong places. She said she did not want to be skinny but wanted to maintain her weight on an even keel at a point where her husband would not consider her "disfigured."

We agreed that her right weight was around the 130 pound mark. I proposed that she go on the 1200-calorie Miracle Diet and to discuss with her physician the possible discontinuance of vitamin supplements. He agreed that the Miracle Diet would provide much more than minimum daily requirements and the vitamins were dropped.

Also dropped were 54 pounds in six months.

When I saw Mrs. T. last she weighed 142 pounds and had decided to continue the 1200-calorie six meal-a-day regime for a while longer. I consider the case "special" because I cannot remember ever *discontinuing* vitamins as a step in going on the Miracle Diet.

There are no specific food requirements in the Miracle Diet so it is flexible and can be adapted to taste and circumstance.

I defy any person to say he or she is a special "case" and cannot:

1. Eat six times a day
2. Eat quantities in keeping with energy expenditure
3. Swing to proteins and away from sweets and starches
4. Make every calorie count in nutrition

The person who is in the habit of little or no breakfast, a sandwich and pie lunch and a "make up for the whole day" dinner is asking for pounds of trouble. Any attempt to justify such a habit as "special" will fall on deaf ears as far as I'm concerned.

J. I. Rodale uses the term "effective calories" to denote calories that are needed by the body at a particular time. He says that the morning calorie will burn up more quickly than the evening calorie, because it has all day to be buffeted about by the activities of the body. Two persons on the same 2000-calorie diet can distribute them differently:

	A	B
MORNING	900	200
NOON	600	600
EVENING	500	1200
	2000	2000

All other conditions equal, he says, A will lose more weight than B.

I agree.

In Chapter 2 we discussed why Miracle Diet breakfasts are solid meals and how five more meals, sized and paced according to the body's energy needs during the day, will create less pressure to store fat.

It is this proper distribution of food intake that must be adhered to as a foundation for the Miracle Diet. On this foundation, you can build any special menu of nourishing foods that special circumstances require.

The Model's Miracle Diet

"I'm a model. I don't like to spend time in the kitchen. I must lose weight fast. I don't like special foods."

Is this person ineligible for the Miracle Diet? On the contrary, she is very eligible.

I have helped a number of models whose requirements generally fit the above. They were not overweight by our standards, but one pound here and two pounds there can be critical by the standards of *Vogue* or other fashion magazines.

Here Is the Model's Miracle Diet A:

BREAKFAST NO. 1   Choice of any fruit—except bananas, grapes, cherries, dried fruits

BREAKFAST NO. 2   1 hard-boiled egg

LUNCH NO. 1   Tuna salad
　　　　　　　Mix small can Tuna (drain oil) with
　　　　　　　1 stick chopped celery
　　　　　　　3 oz. cottage cheese on 1 slice diet toast

LUNCH NO. 2   1 small bran muffin with diet jelly

DINNER NO. 1   3 oz. lean hamburger (broiled)
　　　　　　　½ canned pear
　　　　　　　1 scoop cottage cheese
　　　　　　　1 bed of lettuce

DINNER NO. 2   1 cup skimmed milk
                     1 graham cracker

Since time is of the essence, this diet is less than the 1200 calo-ries that others would start on. In fact, it is under 1000 calories.

If weight loss is not immediate or fast enough, these models are then quickly switched to this 700-calorie Model's Miracle Diet B:

BREAKFAST NO. 1   1 egg, poached, boiled or lightly scrambled

BREAKFAST NO. 2   4 oz. tomato juice
                        1 slice toast (thin)

LUNCH NO. 1   ½ cup cole slaw
                       Broiled flounder with Spanish Sauce
                               or
                       Broiled codfish fillet

LUNCH NO. 2   1 glass skimmed milk

DINNER NO. 1   Baked lean ham
                       ½ boiled potato (med. size)
                       8 stalks asparagus
                               or
                       ⅔ cup spinach

DINNER NO. 2   Broiled grapefruit

The food is easy to shop for. The fish is available in frozen packages. No exotic or special foods. Yet all the proteins, minerals and vitamins for healthful slenderizing are there.

If a 200-pound, five-foot eight-inch man went on this diet, he might lose ten pounds a week which is much too fast. If a 120-pound, five-foot eight-inch model went on this diet she would lose two to three pounds a week for the ten days or two weeks needed to bring her into fashion line.

Her alternative might be to go on dangerous pills. She might get stuck with thyroid-digitalis which does not cause weight re-duction on its own merry loss of appetite. Such pills are being increasingly controlled by the Food and Drug Administration, es-pecially as to misleading labeling. In the past year it has seized over 45 million units of this pill worth about one million dollars on their way from 12 drug companies to any number of obesity clinics. If our model used this drug, she might lose weight, but she would be tampering seriously with her vital organs.

Or our model might go down to a large department store or specialty shop that features weight reducing gadgetry. There she might pause to consider a jogging machine for about $60, a treadmill which reminds me of a hamster's exercise wheel. Or she might try out the feel of a dynabelt at about $70 which is worn under the clothes, battery operated, and sends electronic impulses to the stomach muscles.

Or she might make reservations to go to a $500-a-week spa where her every move and mouthful will be supervised from dawn to dusk. Or she might resort to saunas, steam, or masseuses.

Thousands of firms doing a billion dollar a year business are living off the fat of the land. Little wonder there is increasing concern on the part of government over the efficacy of some of the so-called cures and, in some cases, their outright danger.

Our model has little to worry about in a poached egg or tomato juice or broiled flounder, cole slaw, asparagus, spinach, ham, potato and grapefruit. These are healthful, well-balanced everyday foods.

She is back to work quickly with new accounts and new opportunities to make the right magazine covers.

The Health Spa Miracle Diet

Suppose our model had gone to an exclusive health spa.

Some require total fast. Water, fruit juice, and coffee or tea may be the sole "nourishment."

This can be dangerous, too.

Some people have normal fat. Others have toxic bloat.

When a person with a state of toxic bloat goes on a fast, there can be a toxic crisis. The body has no place to send its poisons. The "garbage pail" is full. Result: Poisons flood the vital organs and the result can be death.

Of course, legitimate health spas provide medical supervision and can head off this type of trouble.

Our model, not being faced with such a problem, is first thoroughly measured on her arrival. Her program while there will be directed not just at taking pounds off but taking them off particular places.

U.S. Department of Agriculture statistics on women ages 20–29 show that there is a trend to slightly larger busts, smaller waists and smaller hips. The increase in busts from 1939 to 1969 went up a trace from 33.97 to 33.99 inches while waists shrank from 26.62 to 25.83 and hips from 37.48 to 36.44.

Figure styles for our model are guided more by fashion and fad than by standard statistics. Her agent may have told her— "take it off the bust and waist, dear." Spa activities would then be aimed in those directions.

But her spa menu would not likely change. Here is a typical example. This is from a spa where many small meals are recognized as a method superior to three larger meals.

The Spa's Miracle Diet

DAY NUMBER ONE

BREAKFAST NO. 1   6 oz. orange juice
1 egg poached, boiled, scrambled (lightly)

BREAKFAST NO. 2   ¾ cup vegetable soup

LUNCH NO. 1   4 oz. broiled codfish fillet
or
4 oz. broiled flounder

LUNCH NO. 2   1 glass skimmed milk mixed with dried milk

DINNER NO. 1   Veal chop broiled
½ cup onions and peas
1 boiled potato medium
⅓ cup applesauce

DINNER NO. 2   2 apricot halves on 1 scoop cottage cheese

DAY NUMBER TWO

BREAKFAST NO. 1   ½ cup canned grapefruit
or
½ fresh grapefruit

BREAKFAST NO. 2	6 oz. orange juice 1 egg, poached, boiled, scrambled 1 slice toast (thin) 1 cup coffee with 1 tsp. sugar
LUNCH NO. 1	¾ cup vegetable soup Spanish omelet
LUNCH NO. 2	1 glass skimmed milk
DINNER NO. 1	Broiled veal chop ½ cup mashed turnips ⅔ cup spinach
DINNER NO. 3	Diet Jello mixed with fresh fruit

Similarity to the regular Miracle Diet menus is apparent. Check it with the 800- and 1000-calorie levels. It is right between at 900 calories.

The Career Girl's Sandwich Diet

Today's pace may make proper dieting difficult. But it is not impossible. I have often been faced with having to make it as *easy* as possible rather than as *effective* as possible.

Here is one way I have solved the problem. It is a Miracle Sandwich Diet, an answer for career girls or business bachelors on the run.

The Miracle Sandwich Diet
Using Diet Bread

BREAKFAST NO. 1	Open grilled cheese using 1 slice bread and 1 oz. American cheese
BREAKFAST NO. 2	1 medium apple (fresh or baked)
LUNCH NO. 1	Using 2 slices Diet Bread Lettuce and tomato and choice of: 1 thin slice turkey ½ individual can of tuna

1 slice thin roast beef
sliced boiled egg (1)

LUNCH NO. 2   1 glass of skimmed milk mixed with 1 tsp. dried milk

DINNER NO. 1   Same as lunch plus choice of fruits (using any fruit except bananas, cherries, grapes, dried fruits)

DINNER NO. 2   2 canned pear halves (without syrup) plus 1 scoop cottage cheese on large lettuce leaf

Be sure to note that diet bread is called for. This is a low-fat, whole wheat bread with maximum nutritional punch per calorie.

I take great pains in "architecting" diets to fit the special needs of special people. It's no fun being fat.

I was interested in this no-fun-to-be-fat idea being recognized recently in a "show biz" report. Comedian jokes about fat people no longer go over according to the report. Apparently people recognize the seriousness of being overweight. It's as sure a killer as cancer can be. And you don't hear any jocularity on that subject.

One exception on the fatso jokes: When roly-poly comedienne Nancy Austin, of the Jimmie Rodgers show, steps on an imaginary scale and says in a "Mae West" voice, "I must have gone a little heavy on the eyeshadow"—she gets laughs.

Mrs. Y. struck me as a bitter woman. She lived alone and ate out frequently. She hated house work, disliked preparing anything for herself, and was a rather undisciplined person.

I suggested the six-meal-a-day Miracle Sandwich Diet, pointing out that there was little preparation involved. I reminded her that her 205 pounds on an average frame would bring health problems. It was only a matter of time.

Frankly, I doubted that I would see her again. But she arrived promptly for her second appointment. There was very little weight loss. "I must admit I was off it for a few days," she confessed. This on again, off again continued for four months during which her craving for fattening food gradually diminished as did her weight. Her lapses grew shorter, and all-in-all she recovered her resolve in time so as not to suffer too severe a set-back. She was genuinely pleased with her new look at 165 pounds and continued the diet on her own thereafter. I doubt whether she will ever become a home body, but she is certainly a happier person today.

The Miracle Rice Diet

Special people need special diets.

Mrs. Elizabeth Hughes, wife of New Jersey's former Governor received much publicity when she successfully brought her weight down from 230 to 130 pounds. She revealed that her diet consisted largely of three ounces of meat or chicken a day, salad without dressing, and a banana (twice a week only). Undoubtedly her being a diabetic had much to do with the nature of the diet.

A physician referred a patient to me who, because of the nature of the illness, he had placed on a rice diet. However, the patient was gaining weight.

Problem: How do you create a special rice diet that will make every calorie count in nutrition?

We tried the following:

800-CALORIE MIRACLE RICE DIET

BREAKFAST NO. 1	½ cup of rice
BREAKFAST NO. 2	½ cup of rice, 3 oz. drained tuna
LUNCH NO. 1	½ cup of rice
LUNCH NO. 2	½ cup of rice
DINNER NO. 1	½ cup of rice, 3 oz. white meat chicken
DINNER NO. 2	½ cup of rice, plus ½ canned pear

This diet is almost completely devoid of salt, so it is an excellent solution to the problem of bloating or puffiness. However, it should not be attempted without the supervision of a physician.

The rice is washed twice before boiling which can be done in fruit juice or unsalted water. There should be another washing after cooking. The rice may be eaten plain, or you may add small portions of any unsweetened fruit except bananas.

Every other meal may include small three-ounce portions of white meat chicken or tuna. No salt may be used, but flavoring may be added using clove, mustard, pepper, onion or horseradish.

Each cooked half cup of white rice has 75 calories. The calorie count of brown rice is slightly higher, but well worth the added minerals and vitamins.

The Miracle Liquid Diet

Another diet that, without reservation, requires the supervision of a physician, but which has had unbelievably quick results in melting away the pounds is a liquid diet.

Most liquid diets confine the gustatory prisoner to two or three basic drinks, three times a day.

This special diet lives up to Miracle Diet principles in that it provides six liquid meals a day and utilizes a diversified list of juices, soups and beverages so as to supply the greatest number of minerals and vitamins.

Don't kid yourself about liquids. They can be fattening. You can get fat just as fast on a liquid diet as you can get thin. Liquids go down fast and easy and then you're ready for another.

However, if you have a disciplined willpower, here are some of the most nourishing types of readily obtainable liquid foods that you can use on the Miracle Liquid Diet; also shown is a typical day:

Tea or coffee with nothing added	no calories
Whole milk	140 "
Skim milk	70 "
Buttermilk	75 "
Apple juice (unsweetened)	100 "
Grapefruit juice (unsweetened)	95 "
Orange juice (unsweetened)	85 "
Tomato juice	45 "
Sauerkraut juice	8 "
Consommé	46 "
Tomato soup	86 "
Bouillon	12 "
Chicken soup	74 "

TYPICAL DAY

BREAKFAST NO. 1   8 oz. whole milk
BREAKFAST NO. 2   1 cup tomato soup

LUNCH NO. 1	1 cup orange juice
LUNCH NO. 2	1 cup buttermilk
DINNER NO. 1	1 cup chicken soup plus 1 cup of whole milk
DINNER NO. 2	Consommé

The typical day shown is a minimum. It is the 600-calorie level. At the 1200-calorie level you may add meals or you may add liquids to the six meals. One man who went from 198 pounds to 167 pounds in one month on this diet at the 1000-calorie level had eight liquid meals a day.

For Vegetarians Only

Your body can extract from vegetables all the minerals and vitamins it needs. You can even get your minimum quota of protein out of them, too, because many contain protein up to 20 percent to 30 percent of their calorie content.

Here are some examples:

VEGETABLE	PROTEIN	FAT	CARBOHY-DRATE	TOTAL CALORIES
Broccoli (1 cup)	16	—	28	44
Chinese cabbage (1 cup)	4	—	20	24
Carrots, raw (6 tbs.)	4	—	20	24
Celery, two stalks	4	—	8	12
Corn, 1 lg. fresh ear	20	18	120	158
Kale (½ cup)	12	9	28	49
Mustard green (½ cup)	12	—	20	32
Peas, green (¾ cup)	28	—	72	100
Spinach, fresh (2 tbs. cooked)	4	—	4	8
Squash, winter (½ cup)	8	—	40	48
Stringbeans, fresh (6 tbs.)	8	—	16	24
Turnips (½ cup)	4	—	16	20

Vegetarians can also find protein in milk—28 protein calories, 72 fat and 40 carbohydrate in one cup of whole milk. Skimmed milk has no fat. Its protein is rated at 28 calories with 40 carbohydrate calories in one cup.

Other vegetarian sources of protein—also about 20 percent—are soybeans, peanuts, and the following cheese:

CHEESE	PROTEIN	FAT	CARBOHY-DRATE	TOTAL CALORIES
Brick (1″× 2″ × ⅛″)	44	135	—	179
Brie (American—				
2½″ × 1¼″ × ½″)	40	99	—	139
Edam (1″ × 3″ × 1″)	52	90	8	150
Gouda (1″ × 2″ × 1″)	20	63	4	87
Gruyere (1″ × 4″ × ⅝″)	28	72	2	102
Limburger				
(3½″ ×4½″ × ½″)	28	81	—	109
Munster				
(3½″ × 4½″ × ½″)	24	81	—	105
Swiss (American—				
4″ × 4″ × ⅛″)	24	63	—	87
Velveeta (4″ × 4″ × ⅛″)	16	45	—	61

Flours favored by vegetarians include soybean flour which is 60 percent protein and gluten flour, 45 percent protein.

When I assist a vegetarian to drop unwanted fat, I find I cannot provide the percentage protein that characterizes the Miracle Diets. Certainly the total amount of protein is adequate and perhaps the lesser amount is in part compensated for by the abundance of other nutrients that fairly burst from the fresh vegetables and salads.

Here Is My Miracle Vegetable Diet

BREAKFAST NO. 1   Celery stalks and fresh mushrooms

BREAKFAST NO. 2   Lettuce ½ head with French dressing (low calorie)

LUNCH NO. 1   Beef tomato and sliced onion with mayonnaise (low calorie)

LUNCH NO. 2   Corn (2 ears) spread butter and salt

DINNER NO. 1   Combine beets, peas, string beans, carrots, tomato and boiled dressing (low calorie)

DINNER NO. 2   Mixed Salad (Make base of crisp lettuce leaves; chop canned French beans, fresh mushrooms, small

> pieces fresh cauliflower, green peas, cold canned asparagus, marinated artichoke, celery stalks. Sprinkle with parsley and sliced radishes.)

Note that absent are sweet corn, lentils, black-eyed peas, sweet potatoes and yams. Heavy in carbohydrates, these would reduce the protein percentage.

Those who adopt this diet, with the consent of their physician, should drink lots of water. They may use lemon or vinegar freely and spices as desired. As to salad dressing, I recommend a zero calorie dressing made from white vinegar, salt, water and pepper. It can be sweetened to taste with an artificial (non-cyclamate) sweetener.

Some vegetarians prefer a fruit diet. No problem. But down go proteins even further:

FRUIT	PROTEIN	FAT	CARBOHY-DRATE	TOTAL CALORIES
Apple (3″ diameter)	4	9	116	129
Apricots (dried 5 halves)	8	—	88	96
Banana (medium)	4	—	80	84
Blueberries (fresh, ¾ cup)	4	9	76	89
Blackberries (fresh, ¾ cup)	8	9	60	77
Cantaloupe (½ medium)	4	—	36	40
Currants (fresh, 1 cup)	8	—	52	60
Grapefruit (½ medium)	4	—	44	48
Grapes, Amer. (4 oz.)	4	9	60	73
Loganberries (fresh, ¾ cup)	4	9	60	73
Mangoes (2 or 3)	4	—	44	48
Nectarines (2)	4	—	36	40
Orange (4″ diameter)	4	—	64	68
Papaya (3″ wedge)	4	—	40	44
Peach (fresh, medium)	—	—	44	44
Pear (fresh, medium)	4	—	64	68
Pineapple (canned, 1 slice)	—	—	60	60
Plum (fresh, large)	—	—	20	20
Raspberries (fresh, 1 cup)	4	9	72	85
Rhubarb (fresh, 1 cup)	4	—	16	20
Strawberries (fresh, 1 cup)	4	9	40	53
Tangerine (medium)	2	—	23	25

When dieting on fruit, fresh varieties are, of course, preferred. If not available, frozen may then be used, but when thawed should be drained of any syrup. Water packed is to be favored over syrup in canned fruit, and syrup should also be drained from canned fruit.

Here Is the Miracle Fruit Diet

BREAKFAST NO. 1   ½ cup canned apricots
                   1 banana

BREAKFAST NO. 2   4 oz. American grapes
                   1 medium pear

LUNCH NO. 1   ¾ cup loganberries
                   1 medium apple

LUNCH NO. 2   ½ cantaloupe
                   1 medium orange

DINNER NO. 1   2 nectarines
                   ¾ cup pineapple

DINNER NO. 2   1 cup strawberries
                   1 peach

This diet runs 800 to 900 calories. It will take weight off miraculously fast. I don't recommend it for general use, but rather for those special people whose physician or daily dietary habits require it.

Other Special Diets

Special people come in all shapes and sizes. And so do their physical needs. Among other types of special diets I have had to prepare are the:

> Low Fat Diet
> Fat-Free Diet
> Fruit and Vegetable Diet
> High Protein—High Fat Diet
> High Protein—Low Fat Diet
> Raw Fruit Diet

Vitality Diet
High Vitamin Diet

I have also prepared and administered, at physicians' requests, the following special diets for special physical conditions:

Gastro-Irritability Diet
Constipation Diet
Acne Diet
Low Cholesterol Diet
Low Salt Diet
Salt-Free Diet
Diuretic Diet
Allergy Diet
Arthritis Diet
High Blood Pressure Diet
Kidney Stone Diet
Anti-Acid Diet
Ulcer Diet
Diabetic Diet
Soft Diet
Heart Disorder Diet
Pre-natal Diet

What we eat, we are.

Our body is shaped, strengthened, restored, adjusted, and re-generated by the foods we consume. Every mouthful needs to be watched. And what an injustice it is to inject into our system sugary, starchy cake, candy, and confections that demand so much of our body and contribute so little.

Such so-called goodies, that would be more appropriately named bad-ies, appear on not *one* diet—special or regular—I have ever seen.

The Person with Gourmet Tastes

Lest you think that special people are only those with special problems, remember that people can also have special gourmet tastes, special hankerings for exotic foods, and other special demands on the other end of the menu spectrum.

I have had a Cordon Bleu-trained amateur chef who would settle for nothing less than the astronomical gastronomical level of shirred eggs and veal kidneys for breakfast, quail for lunch, and crabmeat bouillabaisse for dinner. Interspersed as number two meals were breakfast kippers, stuffed mushrooms, and salmon mousse in aspic.

Since he enjoyed cooking for himself, the trouble dissolved into fun. And since gourmet tastes lean to high protein foods, delicate seasonings and fresh, flavorsome produce, it was much easier to create well-balanced Miracle Diet menus for him than for the vegetarians and others with restricted diets.

A Chinese gentleman, who had succumbed to the Western ways and had a 30-pound paunch to show for it, lost it in six weeks when he went back to preparing his own food and eating in Chinese restaurants.

The Chinese chef, like gourmets around the world, takes great care in the selection of ingredients. Foods must always be fresh, attractive and wholesome to insure the most delectable results.

Chinese cooking preserves the nutritional value of the foods used. The Chinese chef uses a round-bottomed frying pan with a minimum of water. He turns and stirs then puts the cover on to allow the steam to penetrate the food. He adds a little more water, if needed, and soy sauce (cornstarch, too, but we won't mention that), turns and stirs some more and the delicious deed is done.

Apparently the gourmet is here to stay. At a recent forum of grocery manufacturers and packagers held at the Waldorf-Astoria in New York, it was easy to see that the gourmet is alive and eating well in the United States. Gourmet societies and eating clubs are everywhere, and Mr. and Mrs. Average Homeowner are buying imported foods and frozen gourmet dinners more frequently.

The Miracle Diet does not impede the gourmet in any way. And by staying thin, he knows he can go on to eat well another day.

Children as Special People

A recent survey of several thousand households in the midwest reveals that American mothers are feeding their children too much of the wrong types of foods. And many mothers were setting the stage for serious problems for their children later in life.

The wrong foods were the constant snacks, the pizzas, the sugary dry cereals; the ice cream, cake and candy routine; and the cases and cases of bottled soda. Not only are these the wrong foods for well-nourished bodies, but the wrong eating habits for later years.

To compound the error, many mothers were using the wrong foods as rewards for good behavior or withholding wrong foods as a punishment. About 70 percent used food as a tool of parental discipline, thus setting the stage decades from now for the adult to "reward" himself with fattening food.

Children will benefit by following your new Miracle Diet eating practices along with you—and they may retain these wholesome habits for life. This can be a valuable heritage.

Parents are usually responsible for their children's excess poundage. Studies show that if one parent is overweight there is a 50-50 chance the child will be too. If both parents are overweight, the odds increase.

In fact, according to Dr. Jules Hirsch of Rockefeller University, overfeeding children builds fat cells which remain in their bodies throughout life. When later they try to diet, these fat cells may shrink for a time; but soon the body heeds their demands, and the resulting craving for food is almost irresistible. So—the pounds lost are quickly regained.

And to go even further, columnist Francis K. Ichigaya believes that revising a child's diet away from carbohydrates and including more protein will actually affect his growth potential. Over their growing years, he says, a superior diet can add as much as three or four inches to a child's stature.

Miracle Step Nine

Health or environmental problems need not interfere with your going on a six-meal-a-day Miracle Diet. Six meals consisting of highly nutritional foods can be devised for any person and any condition. Create your own health spa right at home or follow the models and Hollywood stars in their special diets. But plan on making minerals and vitamins count just as much as calories for you and your children.

10

Significant Secrets of the Miracle Diet

I have taken a whole book to tell you what is really a very simple story.

It is not an original story. It goes back to the very beginning of man. But much of it surely seems to have been forgotten.

Take this matter of protein. If you talk low carbohydrate diet, you are "controversial." If you talk high protein diet, very few voices are raised in opposition. It appears that the words "low carbohydrate" go against the grain of those who favor a well-balanced diet. What they overlook is the fact that we grow fat on an unbalanced diet.

The first thing the family doctor told an overweight person a generation or two ago was, "Cut out sweets and starches." Controversial? Of course not, you sort of expected him to say just that.

I have dropped the terminology "low carbohydrate diet" because it invites hackles to rise on a few nutritionists who think you mean to cut out carbohydrates entirely. Of course, you know it does not mean this. The Miracle Diet merely restores your proper carbohydrate-protein balance by "cutting out sweets and starches."

It provides you, instead, with the kind of carbohydrates that brim with vitamins and minerals—more carbohydrates than your body needs, abundant carbohydrates to give you all of the quick energy you require. But fewer carbohydrates than we usually eat in this age of snacks, pop, and candy.

Some Problems That Face Miracle Dieters

Why is it that we drift toward carbohydrates and away from proteins?

If you watch cattle grazing in a field, they drift away from scrawny areas where the pasture contains some types of grasses that are not their natural feed, and they move instinctively toward more suitable areas. Tall grass growing in urinated areas is avoided. The bulk and luscious green appearance is by-passed in favor of more nutritional spots and cows constantly risk their necks by reaching through barbed wire fences to reach grasses on the virgin soil along the highway. We probably might drift in more nutritional directions in our supermarkets were it not for the conditioning that we receive to the contrary via advertising, promotion, and packaging.

These pressures are enough to overcome our natural tendencies and to shove us instead in the direction of the morass of cookies, crackers and cakes and away from the minerals and vitamins we were born to live on.

I don't blame it on Madison Avenue. We ask for it. We demand the quick and the easy, little realizing we are asking for "slow death."

Carbohydrates are ready to pop in your toaster and pop in your mouth. Proteins are not.

Then there is the matter of cost. Carbohydrates are a dime for 500 calories. The same amount of protein calories cost a dollar or two.

Many protein foods are priced right out of reach for large low-income families. And in some parts of the less privileged world they are just plain not available.

We hear much about conservation. Yet, one of the major prob-

lems facing the world today is how to supply a burgeoning popula-
tion with sufficient protein foods at a price it can afford.

Scientists on both sides of the Iron Curtain believe that the
Antarctic Ocean may eventually hold the answer. At a recent
symposium on Antarctic biology attended by representatives of the
12 nations engaged in research in Antarctica, the opinion was expressed that krill could supply the additional protein for human
consumption needed by the year 2000.

Krill are crustaceans one or two inches long that help make up
the plankton, or smaller marine life of the ocean. Estimates of
this potential protein source vary from 30 million tons a year to
150 million tons. This compares to a total estimated annual world
fishery production today of 50 million tons.

Yes, it would go a long way to solving the protein problem, but
there are other serious, nutritional problems ahead that must be
solved, too.

Plants synthesize carbohydrates with little, if any, help from the
soil. Given sufficient air, rainfall and sunshine, the bulk and
fattening food value is assured even in the poorest of soils.

However, they need a fertile soil for help in converting these
carbohydrates into amino acids and proteins. They must be able
to get from the soil sulphur, phosphorus, nitrogen and other
materials that make up the protein molecule.

These materials were there in abundance for the first crop
grown on American farms, and the second annual and the third,
even the fiftieth. But some American soil is producing its 100th
crop, some its 200th crop or more. Many materials, like nitrogen,
have been restored through chemical fertilizers. But there are
many more that have not been replaced.

Protein content has been dropping in our wheat. In corn there
has been a drop from 9.5 to 8.5 percent in a brief period of
ten years.

Veterinarians are keenly aware of the effects of depleted soil on
animals. However, the diseases of human beings are seldom traced
back behind the diagnostic names that appear on medical charts
and death certificates.

The answer to this one is not yet in sight. It does not seem
economically possible to properly feed the soil on a large com-

mercial scale. Certainly it is a problem that deserves more of our research resources. And most certainly it is a problem that will get progressively more critical.

The Miracle Diet in a Nutshell

You and I are not going to solve the problems of the world. We do well to solve our own individual problems.

A key problem of ours is how to get rid of unwanted pounds—safely, permanently, easily and fast.

The Miracle Diet is doing it.

How? By providing:

- Six modest meals a day instead of three larger meals, reducing the need for the body to store fat.
- A relatively substantial breakfast in place of "light" breakfasts. This insures adequate blood sugar at the time it is needed and prevents hunger-eating cycles.
- Relatively light dinners to avoid storage of calories during low activity hours at night.
- High protein foods to prevent breakdown of the body's cell replacement and repair processes.
- High mineral foods to insure top level efficiency of the body's vital functions.
- High vitamin foods to continue a youthful tone and bodily vigor.
- Caloric limits that yield a safe but substantial weight loss until normal weight is reached.
- Enjoyable foods to minimize willpower and create a permanent new way of pleasurable eating rather than just another, possibly injurious, on again–off again diet.
- High energy foods that insure an exuberance and dynamic energy while you slenderize.

This is the Miracle Diet in a nutshell.

Mrs. M., an attractive woman and the mother of two children, seemed to always have had a tendency to being over-

weight. Married life seemed to make this all the more noticeable because, as she put it, she was "very contented."

At five feet two inches she weighed 158 pounds, close to 40
pounds of excess baggage. She warned me that she had tried
going on diets before but never had the willpower to follow
through. "I love entertaining," she explained. "We have people over several times a week. I guess I'm a show-off. I get a
kick out of preparing different gourmet specialties and then
accepting the raves." She also got a kick out of eating her own
preparations. In fact, when the guests left, she polished off the
leftovers.

The six-meal-a-day Miracle Diet made one immediate
change in Mrs. M. Where she skipped breakfast, she now had
two. It resulted in less appetite at night.

Little else was changed, because her dinner no. 1 and dinner
no. 2 were still vehicles for entertaining. We worked out a
number of Miracle Diet recipes that were high in food value,
low in calorie value, and were tasty and different. The first
week she reported her guests were "enchanted" with Yum
Patou, a Thailand cocktail hour favorite that is basically tuna
fish on long leaves of endive lettuce with a few peanut bits
sprinkled on top. (The tuna fish is mixed with lots of lemon
juice and a touch of hot pepper.)

From then on it was easy rolling off the fat. Her guests
were doubly impressed because they, too, were weight conscious. She stayed with the diet and in four months was down
to 120.

Don't underestimate the important effect of six meals a day. It
can make all the difference between losing weight and not losing
weight. A young woman in her early twenties came to me after she
had gained 17 pounds lying in bed nursing injuries to her neck
and leg in an automobile accident. Prior to the accident she
weighed 128. Now she was 145 and being five feet five with a
small frame she did not carry the extra pounds gracefully and was
eager to return to her normal weight. She tried pills, but they had
undesirable effects. Now she was on a diet, but it was not working.

I examined the diet she was on. The foods were nutritional,
balanced and calorie-wise within the proper limits. I asked her to

split up her breakfast into two sittings, and ditto her lunch and dinner. "Don't change a thing else," I said. She looked at me with a dubious expression, but promised to try.

It worked. Six meals a day consisting of the identical foods brought her down two pounds that week where she had not lost in weeks of trying before. In two months the unwanted fat was gone.

Six meals a day is a critical aspect of the Miracle Diet. Skip a meal and you can gain, not lose.

Skip Breakfast and You Raid the Kitchen at Night

When you talk to overweight people day in and day out as I do, you begin to see they have similar eating habits: they eat fast; they favor carbohydrates; they skip breakfast; they eat big meals at night that go on and on from one snack to another.

One man admitted he often got up three times during the night to raid the refrigerator.

Let's talk about that man. He had a cup of coffee in the morning and he was on his way to the office. I accepted him as a client on one condition: that he would eat a steak every morning for two weeks before he left for the office.

There was a method in my apparent madness. He was an inveterate steak eater. So I used steak as bait to break through his resistance to eating in the morning. I knew he was not going to sit down to two poached eggs on toast just at my say so.

It pulled the rug right out from under him—the rug that goes down the hall leading to his refrigerator.

He found that he had an appetite a few hours after the steak so I hooked him on a second breakfast, albeit somewhat lighter. He found he was more interested in lunch. I talked him into splitting that into two sittings, the second at three P.M.

By the time dinner came around he could hardly work up an appetite for it. Munching in the evening was out. He was full. And no more night forays.

What about his weight? It started to drop just by the change in his eating habits.

He had finally gotten off the blood-sugar roller coaster "ride" that his no breakfast habit was taking him on. I don't think he ever realized how I used steak to "bribe" him.

But he knows the importance of breakfasts to stay slender.

I have to resort to all sorts of devices to get overweight people to eat breakfasts. I remember one woman who had gained weight because she ate heavily to appease her nervous tension over her 17-year-old son who had been in some trouble. Her lunches and dinners had become twice as large since the incident, but no breakfasts. I got her on five meals a day, but no breakfast. It would be a miracle if I got her on six. One day, after no weight loss progress, I asked her if she ate breakfasts on vacation in the country. Yes, that was different she said. It was my break-through. She agreed to play a "vacation" game for a week. That week was all I needed to change her habit.

Snack If You Wish and Lose Weight

Recently I read a published interview with the head of one of the largest bakeries in the United States. Sales were mounting steadily and he attributed the greater volume of crackers being sold to the fact that people were giving up three solid meals a day and eating five or six half meals a day. He called it a new movement.

If he is right, I applaud the new movement. If any client wishes to increase the six meals a day of the Miracle Diet to eight or ten or even twelve, he or she is welcome.

But not crackers.

All I insist on is emphasis on proteins and an honest count on total calories.

Naturally you are not going to lose weight going from hamburger stand to pizza parlor eight times a day.

You will lose weight going from an egg to yogurt to tuna fish to bouillon to salad to liver to skimmed milk to a tangerine eight times a day.

Eight or ten well-planned snacks a day can be better for you than three rich squares a day.

I am all for that kind of snacking.

Excerpts from the Miracle Diet Mailbag

It is a most rewarding experience when one sees the pounds slowly, but surely, disappearing.

I feel and look much better. For the first time I have the feeling that I won't gain it back.

It doesn't pay to be fat. I know because up until the end of 1963 I never had a weight problem. I weighed under 125 and all of a sudden I gained over 25 pounds in a short period of time. I've been sorry for six long years. One feels like a new person when the pounds are shed. I feel better, but I still won't be completely satisfied until 15–20 pounds more are lost.

I am able to stick to this diet for longer periods of time, even though I have encountered set-backs. I get back on. I feel better, look well and I am on my way to reaching my goal.

I am less tired, more interested in doing things.

I can walk long distances now without that backache.

I enjoy looking in the mirror now.

I have more energy even though I sleep less. My romantic life has improved. Girls look at me.

Thinking Habits Can Be as Fattening as Eating Habits

Recently a very unusual test was held at Columbia University. Participating were about 40 fat young men and 40 lean young men. They were not told the true purpose of the test: to see if a full stomach and fear of getting hurt physically would deter the overweight boys from overeating. Instead they were told that this was a taste test for different kinds of crackers.

Each was seated alone in a cubicle with five bowls of crackers. Some were wired with electrical shock apparatus and told they would occasionally get a painful shock while tasting the crackers. Others were given roast beef sandwiches first.

The lean men ate very few of the crackers. The fear of shock in some cases, the full stomachs in others confined their cracker eating to just enough to taste the difference.

The overweight young men gorged themselves on the crackers. Neither the fear of shock nor the absence of hunger hindered their snacking. Conclusion: something besides the usual factors trigger eating by those who are overweight.

But what does this triggering?

The answer, in my opinion, is above the mouth, not below it. It is in the conditioning of the mind.

In many cases this conditioning is performed by parents who reward children with food. In other cases this conditioning is performed by ourselves later in life but not totally unrelated to youth's problems.

They say that inside every overweight person is a slender one trying to get out. The reason the slender one cannot get out, in my opinion, is because underneath all those layers of corpulence is an emotional magnet.

This mental factor attracts food because eating acts as a tranquilizer and allays the pain of that emotional factor, whatever be its nature. A child cries because it is frightened, insecure, hungry, lonely, bored, and so forth. A plastic "pacifier" is placed in the child's mouth and the crying stops.

The security brought by a nipple in the infant's mouth is repeated later when the three-year-old sucks on a "pacifier." That same feeling of security is repeated decades later by food, cigarettes, or chewing gum in adult mouths.

Whatever needs pacifying varies from person to person. It is not a severe emotional problem, like a neurosis or a paranoia. It can be something very minor. But it is still annoying or unpleasant. It causes a feeling of not being at ease.

Food restores the ease, conditioned by the days of infancy.

What can we do about it?

Substitute a stronger conditioning in its place. For instance, if we had an absolutely irresistible urge to be sexually attractive that over-rode all other urges, when the minor, unpleasant emotional problem nudged us to eat, it would get nowhere. It would turn to some other outlet. Instead of eating it might cause talking, walking, reading or some other "pacifying" activity.

The stronger conditioning is easy to come by. I described the method of relaxation and thinking thin some chapters back. You can add more voltage to the reconditioning. All you do is:

Relax deeper
Visualize more vividly
Practice longer and more frequently

When you "visualize," what you are actually doing is using your mental power to plant a thought-form in your subconscious mind. It is like programming a computer. It *must* work.

No amount of willpower can prevent a properly visualized thought from working. When you visualize that leftover piece of apple pie in the refrigerator, your willpower might prevail for five minutes, ten minutes, but eventually you must get up and satisfy that thought-form.

When you visualize your slender image as vividly as that apple pie, nothing will interfere with your satisfying *that* thought-form.

Form a clear mental image. A fuzzy picture of the end result will not compete with the vivid picture of the apple pie. See yourself in the dresses you cannot wear now or in those good suits you had to put into mothballs. See all the attractive details of the new person you will be.

By giving your mind this kind of a blueprint, you are overcoming past conditionings that have been supplying your mind with a different kind of a blueprint—a pacifying blueprint with food as the sedative.

Something happened to Linda L. way back in early childhood that made her equate happiness to chocolate cake. What it was we will probably never know, but it was my problem to find some way to neutralize this conditioning. Linda, at 15, was average height but a good 50 pounds above her normal weight.

When she came home from school she would consume a half of a chocolate cake, and more of it would disappear before the day was over. She liked cheese and potatoes, too, but if there was no chocolate cake in the house you could be sure there would be a very unhappy Linda.

On a diet, Linda would be very deceptive. She said she wasn't indulging, but she was. She did not like school lunches so she usually packed her own sandwich and thermos of soup. There may not be any chocolate cake tucked away there today, but did you check her purse?

Because Linda's penchant for chocolate cake seemed to come during and after school, I sensed that she was compensating for a feeling of inadequacy. I let her fool me on the dieting while I went to work to build up her ego.

Instead of talking food, we talked Linda. We did some imaging exercises that formed new self-images. She began to see herself as a capable, popular person. Self-confidence was the key. We built that higher and higher through suggestion and imaging and other mental reconditioning processes.

Then I "rang" in her weight. She was now primed to be more conscious of her extra pounds. She wanted more dates and seemed anxious to share the fun of talking with her girl friends about the boys they knew.

You could write the end of this story. That's correct. The portions of chocolate cake became smaller and less frequent. Linda lost weight. Soon she equated chocolate cake to an insecure person she had now outgrown.

Anybody can use reconditioning to get rid of unwanted habits, attitudes and personality quirks. It's a simple do-it-yourself procedure: Just relax, quiet the mind and give yourself either verbal or visualized "commands."

Use the detailed instructions provided in Chapter 7. Vary the images to suit your personal needs.

It is important to do this. The Miracle Diet may be more appetizing than others, more satisfying and more successful, but if there is an underlying unconscious force pushing you off it which is stronger than your conscious willpower to stay on, all these dietary advantages will be lost in the mental scuffle.

Six Meals Are as Easy as Three

This Miracle Diet story is being told by every person who has ever been on it. Thousands of men and women are describing their "painless," "easy to stay on," "never hungry," "energy plus," "fastest ever" dieting experience.

Conversation is a two-way street and they are getting some back talk.

"I don't have the time or inclination to fix three meals a day, you'll never get me to fix six." This is probably the most frequent objection I have heard. Yet it melts away as soon as they actually get started.

Six small meals a day are actually just as easy to prepare as three:

- Each meal is smaller
- There are fewer items
- Some meals can be prepared at the same time as the previous meal
- Many Miracle foods need no preparation
- Many are "portable" and can be taken with you for later use
- Most Miracle foods are in every supermarket
- Three of the six meals are as easy as taking a coffee break, afternoon tea, or late snack
- Six meals a day are easier on a weight-laden body

The Most Important Ingredient in the Miracle Diet

Every now and then somebody comes up with a theory about obesity that hints at total blamelessness of all overweight people. There was the era of the glands. Now enter the antibodies.

It appears that a group of physicians who ran tests on 1500 grossly obese patients in St. Louis has discovered that their bodies' thyroxin was being prevented from circulating by antibodies.

Thyroxin, if you recall, is the hormone manufactured in the thyroid gland that assists in regulating the metabolic rate. With thyroxin's transportation blocked, the rate slowed down and energy not burned was stored as fat. When the physicians used chemicals to force the thyroxin through the blood-stream despite the antibodies, weight was lost.

Fewer than 10 percent of overweight people can blame organic glandular malfunction. I admire the findings of these physicians, but quite likely they were discovering something that might be a causative factor in "grossly obese" cases, but 90 percent of the people who want to lose 10 to 100 pounds and regain youth and energy and good looks are almost certainly suffering not from antibodies, but from food.

The food they are suffering from is food that fattens them without feeding them—the sugars and starches; the sterile, processed fools; the food grown on overcultivated, depleted soils.

Those who discover nutritious food discover a revitalized way of life. Some go overboard in raving about the accomplishments of vitamins, minerals and proteins. They speak of growing new hair, sharpening eyesight, and curing every ill you can name.

All I claim for these nutrients is a normal body.

They are what your body expects. Without them unbalances occur, including a scale that reads "tilted." With them, you radiate with that natural indescribable glow that other people find irresistible.

But without the most important ingredient of all, all of this cannot occur.

That ingredient is you.

You must recognize that those three extra inches around your middle are a threat to your happiness, your health, and your life expectancy.

You must resolve that you will do what needs to be done—first and foremost: cut calories.

You must acknowledge that cutting is not enough and only leads to discouraging weight loss and weight regain cycles.

You must understand the advantage of six meals a day over three, of proteins over carbohydrates, and of minerals and vitamins over foods that are denatured or depleted of these.

The rest will be easy.

You will be on the Miracle Diet before you can screw up your willpower. You will hardly recognize it as a diet because you will not be starving yourself. You will not have those familiar hunger pangs or those periods of total depletion or those miserable moments where you decide you cannot "take it" anymore. You will not hit the refrigerator and make up for lost time.

All that will be a nightmare of past diets.

Instead you will enjoy the blessings I promised you: A fast,

SIGNIFICANT SECRETS OF THE MIRACLE DIET

painless weight loss. More vigor and energy in your daily activities. Improvements in your business, your family life and your social life. A youthful, glowing look that will lighten your heart, bring you new friends, and build high levels of confidence. Vigorous good health and years added to your life.

Think about it . . . on your way to the supermarket.

Index

Index

Brain, effect of diet on, 161
Bran cereal, 57, 73
Bread and grains, 164–166, 184
  diet bread, 213
  whole wheat, 213
Breakfast, 36–37
  importance of, 53–54, 229–230
Brewer's yeast, 57, 166, 169, 181
Brothers, Joyce, 179

C

Caffeine, 182
Calcium, 57, 201, 202
Calcium disodium, 163
Calories:
  avoiding empty, 156, 207
  in cheese, 159–160
  content of fish and meat, 158
  daily consumption, 37–38
  definition, 37
  different types of, 63
  distribution during day, 207–208
  effect of excess, 49–52
  limits for each meal, 116–117, 156,
    207–208
  Miracle Diets, 117–119
  in natural foods, 60–63
  utilization diagrams, 39–48
*Canadian Medical Association Jour-
  nal,* 64
Cantaloupes and prosciutto, 124
Carbohydrates, 24, 25, 187, 224–227
  low carbohydrate diets, 224–225
Castor oil, 181
Cell regeneration, 57, 180, 185, 191
Cheese:
  calorie content, 159–160, 217
  cottage, 159–160
  fluffy cheese dip, 124
  protein content, 217
  savory cream cheese custards, 139–
    140
Chemical additives, 162–163, 181
Chicken:
  breasts Amandine, 129
  breasts with artichokes, 141
  chicken livers, 134, 140–141
  chicken paprika, 131–132

Children:
  diets for, 221–222
  overweight, 175
  rewarding with food, 67, 232
Chinese Chow Mein, 135
Chinese cooking, 221
Chinese egg drop soup, 126–127
Cholesterol, 26, 185
Choline, 198
Coffee and tea, 182–183
Coffee breaks, 36
Columbia University, 231–232
Conditioning to loose weight, 174–
  179, 231–234
Copper, 201, 202
Corn oil, 181
Cornell University, 64
Cosmetics, 181
Crabmeat, deviled with mushrooms,
  139
Cream, non-dairy, 183
Cyclamates, 19–20, 163

D

Dairy products, 57, 62, 159
Davis, Adele, 163
DDT, 163
Dehydrators, 20
Deodorants, 181
Depression, 65
Desserts, 148–153
  apple-pear Betty, 151
  Aruba whip, 153
  baked honey pears, 152
  cantaloupe deluxe, 151
  creamy rhubarb, 152
  Drifting Island, 148
  fancy brown rice pudding, 153
  fruit medley, 150
  heavenly baked bananas, 153
  honey custard, 152
  honey pumpkin pudding, 148
  jellied wine, 149–150
  melon delight, 150
  minted pineapple with coconut,
    151
  no-cook applesauce, 149
  nut cake, 149

Schedule of meals (Cont.)
rate of calorie consumption, 37–38
six meals a day, 36 (*See also* Six
meals a day)
Seeds and nuts, 73, 165, 195
Self-hypnosis, 176–177, 231–234
Sesame seeds, 195
Sexual behavior, 191–196
effect of vitamins, 196–201
glands, 193–195
meal frequency and, 191–192
minerals and, 201–203
proteins and, 192–193
Shipman, Dr. William G., 52
Shopping lists, 115
Shrimp:
appetizers, 123
charcoal broiled shrimp, 140
chinese shrimp salad, 146
consommé, 127
shrimp scampi, 142
Six meals a day, 19
advantages of, 21–22
basic schedule, 38–39
for better health, 26–31
effect on blood sugar, 23–35
importance of first and last meal, 53–55
to improve health, 26–29, 31
to lose weight, 21–24, 26–29
psychological advantages, 29
secret behind, 21–24
sexual behavior and, 191–193
size of meal, 38, 51–53
weight loss due to, 10, 234–235
Skin and hair, 160, 180–181, 236
effect of diet, 180–181
Smoking habit, 176
Snacks, 36, 230
Sodium, 201, 203
Sodium benzoate, 163
Soft drinks, low-calorie, 19
Soils, effect on nutrients, 179, 184, 226–227, 236
Soups, 125–128
Chinese egg drop, 126–127
creamy Venetian soup, 128
hamburg, 127
hearty garlic soup, 125

Soups (Cont.)
icy vegetable, 127
Italian clam soup, 126
salmon bisque, 128
shrimp consommé, 127
spinach, 126
summer salad soup, 126
Soybeans, 67, 165
Special diets, 19, 206–222
fruit diets, 219
health spa diet, 210–212
liquid diets, 215–216
for models, 208–212
rice diet, 214–215
sandwich diet, 212–214
vegetable diets, 216–219
Spices and herbs, 122
Subconscious, reconditioning, 176–179, 233
Sugar, refined, 67–68, 168, 181, 183
Summer camps for overweight teen-agers, 29
Sunflower seeds, 165, 195
Sweet tooth syndrome, 23, 67–68
Sweetbreads, 73, 135
Sweeteners, artificial, 19–20
Sweets, craving for, 23, 67–68

T

Tea and coffee, 182–183
herb teas, 182–183
Tension, 65
Thiamin, 67, 162, 197
Thyroid glands, 193–195, 235
Thyroxin, 235
Tomatoes:
cocktail, 124
eggs baked in, 141–142
sauced tongue, 142
scrambled eggs and, 128–129
stuffed, 134
summer salad soup, 126
Tongue, food value, 73, 142

V

Veal
celery sticks wrapped in, 143–144
chops supreme, 129